Creative Skits
FOR YOUTH GROUPS

Randy Fishell
and
Greg Dunn

BAKER BOOK HOUSE
Grand Rapids, Michigan 49516

Nonprofit organizations using these skits may reproduce
copies for participants without further permission.

Copyright 1987 by Randy Fishell and Greg Dunn

ISBN: 0-8010-3533-3

Second printing, March 1988

Printed in the United States of America

To Diana,
who continues to love her husband
in spite of his obsession
with shrink wrap.
—DGD

To Greg's parents,
who foolishly thought they could make
him a contributing member of society.
—RSF

Acknowledgements

Our friends are, for the most part, a bright group. Some of them even helped develop portions of this book. In particular the authors wish to thank:

> Garren Dent
> Marcos Chavez
> Alvun Baker
> Ted Hessel
> Belinda Cordell
> Tony Krause
> Ivan Chavez
> Richard Bahlmann

We would also like to thank one of our favorite college English professors, Dr. Joyce Rochat, who cannot be held accountable for the material within these pages.

Contents

    Preface   9
1. Life Preserver, Anyone?   11
2. Critical Condition   19
3. Whatever Happened to Sin?   25
(or "Dragnet" Revisited)
4. Long Distance   37
5. Change-O-Rama   43
6. Patent Approved   51
7. A Quaint Little Custom   59
(A live "slide" show on appreciation)
8. Sin-ema   65
9. Backstabbers   71
10. The Health Nuts   79
11. The Blind Optometrist   83
12. The Factory   89

Preface

Creative communication. One could ascribe this term to the inventive efforts of a Guglielmo Marconi or Alexander Graham Bell. From another viewpoint, Paul Harvey's approach to news commentary lends itself to such a description. It would be unusual, however, for anyone to suggest the aforementioned phrase reminds him of God.

But on more than one occasion the Almighty demonstrated that He is indeed the creative communicator *par excellence*. A good example is the method He used in conveying the ten commandments at Mount Sinai. Here, the Creator combined both sight and sound as he employed thunder, lightning, trumpets, and fire in this dramatic presentation of eternal truth. (Exod. 20)

Creative communication of the gospel through drama is what this book is all about. The skits are fun for young people to perform. Besides containing touches of humor, they provide significant insight into the Christian way of life. The props are simple, and the scripts are written in an easy-to-learn style. They may be used for discussion starters or for feature presentations at youth gatherings. After a young person has seen or performed one of these skits, the message will not soon be forgotten.

Randy Fishell
Greg Dunn

1
Life Preserver, Anyone?

For some people, accepting the gift of salvation is a hard thing to do. They make excuses, and put it off, waiting for the right time. Unfortunately, for many that time never comes.

On board the cruise ship *World's End*, you'll encounter some of the most common excuses people make for not accepting Christ's gift. Some, because they've heard it all before, are content to simply ride with the tide. Others don't want to take the plunge until someone else goes first. Those excuses work until the ship begins to sink and the waves come crashing in. That's when it's good to know that there is a life preserver close at hand.

Characters

Narrator
P.A. announcer (offstage)
Henry Eaton, restaurateur
Fred Stockman, investment broker
Eleanor La Tour, world traveler
Mary Singleton, divorcée
John Smith, warehouse supervisor
Captain

Props

5 lawn chairs (both chaise lounges and regular)
Appropriate cruise attire (cameras, sunglasses, etc.)
Table (for drinks)
2 cans of pop
2 drinking glasses
4 life preservers (can be made from poster board if necessary)
Suntan lotion

The action takes place on the Burrito Deck, where the passengers are busy preparing for a day of sun and relaxation.

Narrator: Most of us have grown up believing that nothing in life comes free. But that theory just doesn't hold water when it comes to the gift of salvation.

There are many excuses for not accepting this gift. But when the ship begins to sink and the waves come crashing in, it's good to know that there's a life preserver close at hand.

P.A. Announcer: We'd like to take this opportunity to welcome you aboard the cruise ship *World's End*. If you need anything during your stay aboard ship, please feel free to contact any of the pursers or the cruise director. We have various recreational facilities, and we would like you to enjoy them at your leisure. In addition, for those who wish to participate, an aerobics class will be meeting on the Burrito Deck every morning at 6:30 sharp. *(The passengers "boo" at this suggestion.)* Thank you. Enjoy your cruise!

Henry: *(Spreading out towel, disgruntled.)* The one thing I *don't* need is to get up at 6:30 in the morning and start flapping my wings like a chicken.

Fred: I'm with you, pal. If I work up a sweat, it's going to be from worshiping that great ball of fire in the sky. Speaking of that, could I borrow some suntan lotion?

Henry: Sure. *(Hands him the lotion.)* By the way, my name's Henry Eaton. I own Eaton's Eatery over in Buffalo Springs.

Fred: Hey, I've been there! You've got a great deep-dish pizza. Fred Stockman here. *(The two shake hands.)* I'm in securities myself.

Henry: Well, I'm in the food business, not psychiatry. I'm afraid I can't help you with your insecurity.

Fred: I don't think you understand. I'm in *securities*—you know, investing, Wall Street, and all that.

Henry: Oh, I've got ya!

Eleanor: *(Boldly.)* Did you hear that, Mary? That handsome man is a stockbroker. I'll bet *he* would be a good provider. *(To Fred.)* Hello, there! I'm Eleanor La Tour, and this is my friend Mary

12   Creative Skits for Youth Groups

Singleton. *(Mary nods hello.)* Mary is recently divorced. I thought a cruise would help get her mind off things. But I had no idea we'd be so lucky as to end up sitting next to such eligi—I mean, "eloquent" men.

Henry: *(Sarcastically to Fred.)* Yeah, I always did pride myself on my electrocution of the English language.

Fred: *(To women.)* It's nice to meet you both. And is this gentleman *your* husband, Ms. La Tour? *(Gestures toward John, who has been casually taking in the conversation.)*

Eleanor: *(Teasing.)* Not yet!

Fred: In that case, allow me to introduce myself. *(Reaches over to shake hands with John.)* I'm Fred Stockman, and this is Henry Eaton. *(Henry shakes John's hand.)* I believe you may have caught these ladies' names in passing.

John: *(Shyly.)* Yes, I did. It's nice to meet you all. I'm John Smith.

Eleanor: My, what an unusual name. Is it Bohemian?

John: No, I don't think so. It's actually a fairly common name.

Henry: So, John Smith, what exactly do you do for a living? Not to sound smug, but it must be something rather financially rewarding. These cruises don't exactly fall out of the sky!

John: The truth is, this cruise *did* kind of fall out of the sky for me. I won it.

Fred: Oh? How?

John: Well, until last week I was a loading dock worker at Regal Supply Company. The management there got the idea of holding a contest for the best company money-saving suggestion. The prize was this cruise.

Henry: Congratulations. What exactly was this prize-winning suggestion?

John: It was just a little common sense, really. I figured if we had a computer in the warehouse, we'd have a lot better control of our inventory. Mr. Olson thought the idea was great, promoted me to warehouse supervisor, and told me I had won the contest. So, here I am.

Life Preserver, Anyone?

Eleanor: It all seems brilliant to me. Are you married?

John: No, ma'am, it's just me and Bob Barker, my beagle. It's hard to believe, but I kind of miss that little rascal already.

Eleanor: Oh, Mary just loves puppy dogs, don't you Mary?

Mary: *(Sarcastically.)* Almost as much as brussels sprouts.

Eleanor: *(Disgusted.)* Well!

Fred: *(Looking behind, toward harbor.)* Hey, how about that! I didn't even realize we'd been moving. We're already out so far from shore that you can just barely see the Statue of Liberty!

Henry: Well, that's plenty far enough for me to begin doing what I came to do. I don't know about the rest of you, but I'm ready to kiss Miss Liberty goodbye and get down to some serious relaxing.

(They all agree. John follows their lead. They assume their individual relaxation positions. Some put on sunglasses, one puts a newspaper over his head while stretched out on a chaise lounge, etc. Since John didn't really bring anything to do, he just sits back and relaxes.)

P.A. Announcer: Ladies and gentlemen, your attention please. It appears that we have developed a problem in the boiler area of the ship. Please do not panic. The *World's End* is well-prepared for emergency evacuation. *(The only passenger who becomes concerned is John.)* Your Captain will personally assume the responsibility for seeing that every passenger is provided with a life preserver. There are enough for everyone on board. Please remain where you are until the Captain arrives to provide for your needs.

Henry: I've heard about this kind of entertainment. I think we're supposed to pretend like it's really happening. If I hadn't had to close the restaurant last night, I might play along. But I'm bushed.

John: You mean you don't think they're serious? The ship isn't really sinking?

Fred: I can see you're not up on the latest in games. You see, the idea is to make you feel like it's a life-and-death situation that you're faced with. I can remember when *I* would have reacted the same way you are. But I guess I've kind of gotten used to hearing about this type of thing.

Mary: *(Depressed.)* In a way it might be kind of nice if it *were* sinking. That would be *one* way to get over losing my husband. *(Lamenting.)* If only I had been a better wife. . . .

John: I don't understand! The announcement sounded as if they were trying to tell us that we're actually going down!

Fred: Technology, my boy.

Eleanor: My! You seem to know a lot! Your wife is a very lucky woman!

Fred: Oh, I'm not. . . . Skip it.

John: Well, I'm sorry, but *I* think the announcement was for real! I'm. . . .

(The Captain appears with the life preservers.)

Henry: Hey, Fred. Get a load of the props. He looks like a real seafarer!

Fred: Yeah, he does, doesn't he? *(Grows serious.)* And I think I know why. He *is* the captain of this ship. I remember seeing him when I boarded. *(To Captain.)* Do you mean there really *is* an emergency, Captain?

(The others sit up in their chairs and begin to take notice.)

Captain: *(Anxious but in control of the situation.)* I'm afraid there is. The ship is going down. *(Others become more concerned.)* But there is no need to panic. Anyone who wants a life preserver will be given one. But we must hurry. Who would like to be first? *(Pauses, then to Mary.)* Ma'am, would you accept a life preserver?

Mary: *(Surprised.)* Me? But why should I be first? What about all of these people? Any one of them is twice the person I am. I'm the one who couldn't even hang on to her husband. Maybe if I'd been there when he needed me, I wouldn't be *here* trying to forget the past. No, give them to the others. I'm the last person who deserves a life preserver.

Captain: *(Disappointed.)* I can't force you to accept one, but please reconsider. *(To Henry.)* How about you, sir? Would you accept a life preserver?

Henry: Well, I guess you *are* serious. Sure, I'll take a life preserver. *(Reaches for wallet.)* How much are they?

Captain: Life preservers are free.

Henry: Come on. If you don't take Visa or American Express, I'll give you cash. Now how much does the life preserver cost?

Captain: *(Gently.)* The price has already been paid. It's yours for the asking.

Henry: *(Indignantly.)* I'm sorry, but I didn't make it in the restaurant business by accepting charity. I got where I was by hard work, not by freeloading. No, sir *(puts wallet away)*, if I can't pay you for it, I don't want it! *(Folds arms.)*

(John is amazed at all of the refusals but says nothing yet.)

Captain: *(To Eleanor, almost pleading.)* Ma'am, how about you? The ship is going down, and time is of the essence. Would you *please* accept a life preserver?

Eleanor: *(Uncertain.)* Well, I'd like to, but I don't see anyone else accepting a life preserver. I'm going to play it safe and wait until someone else takes the plunge.

Fred: Well, maybe nobody else wants one, but *I* do! *(To Captain.)* Wait right there! I'll just run and get my investment portfolio and be right with you.

Captain: *(Quickly.)* I'm sorry, but there's no time for that. Just accept the life preserver and. . . .

Fred: *(Interrupting.)* Oh, no! I'm not leaving this ship without that portfolio. That little pack of facts is what put me on Wall Street. Why, I'd be sunk without it. No sir, if I can't take it with me, I'm not going!

Captain: *(Anxiously.)* Isn't there *anyone* who will accept a life preserver? *Anyone?*

John: *(Pauses, looks around.)* I will. *(The other passengers shake their heads disapprovingly. John becomes more sure of himself.)* Yes, I'll take a life preserver. *(Goes over to accept one.)* I don't understand why no one else is taking one, but it seems to me that it's the only sensible thing to do. *(The Captain hands him a life preserver.)*

Henry: It's freeloaders like him that rock the boat for the rest of us.

Fred: Well, it's his own choice. If he comes up a loser, he'll have nobody to blame but himself. Personally, I only take stock in a sure thing.

Mary: Let him go. He'll get what he deserves. *(Dejected.)* I did.

Eleanor: Since only one person has taken a life preserver, it must not be the right thing to do.

Captain: Won't *anyone* else accept my offer? It's free, and it's the only way to safety! *(All mumble and shake their heads no. The Captain then turns to John and speaks.)* We can't wait any longer. Follow me and I'll show you the way. *(Both exit.)*

(All are silent for a brief period, then Eleanor finally breaks the ice.)

Eleanor: *(Nervously, to Fred.)* So, Mr. Stockman, you being an expert financial advisor, would you suggest investing in the *World's End* cruise line?

Fred: No, I suddenly have a sinking feeling that this cruise line may go under.

Eleanor: Oh, dear.

Henry: Come, come now. All of this talk is getting me down. Let's get some of that old spirit back. After all, this may be the last cruise we ever go on! *(He reaches over and picks up a drinking glass.)* I propose a toast. *(The others now reach for their glasses and pop cans.)* To the *World's End*. May she soon reach her destination. Bottoms up, everyone!

(The action freezes as Fred and Henry touch glasses.)

Suggested Scripture

Psalm 18:2; Isaiah 55:1; Titus 2:11

2
Critical Condition

Some people make their living by being critical. There are theater critics, literary critics, and art critics, just to name a few. And then there are others who do not get paid for criticizing others but do it anyway!

When a person unduly criticizes others, it is usually because there is something about himself that he is unhappy with. Before we criticize someone else, it pays to look at ourselves first. It could be that we are just a step away from being in "critical condition"!

Characters

Surgeon
Intern
Nurse
Anesthesiologist
Patient
2 Offstage speakers

Props

Crutch
Matches
Whip
Mirror
Saw
Guitar pick
Hair pick
Balloon
Mask (surgical type)
A table on which to place the patient for the operation. (A sheet covers the table.)
Appropriate attire for medical personnel

Just prior to the skit the patient is placed underneath the sheet. The objects have previously been hidden there. The skit begins with the surgeon and his intern being paged to the operating room.

Offstage Speaker 1: Doctors Wilson and Wiley to surgery. Doctors Wilson and Wiley, please go to surgery.

(The surgeon and his intern enter.)

Intern: So, Doctor, how serious is the patient's illness?

Surgeon: It's very serious, I'm afraid.

Intern: Is it terminal?

Surgeon: No, it's much worse. He's in critical condition!

(Their attention now turns to the patient who is lying motionless on the operating table.)

Intern: Doctor, the patient doesn't seem to be experiencing any of the usual symptoms.

Patient: *(Head pops up and he inspects the surgeon.)* Hey, Doc, where d'ya get them shoes?

Surgeon: *(Startled.)* As I recall, I bought them at Father and Son Shoes.

Patient: Well, let me give you a word of advice, Doc. It just ain't you. It looks like you've got enough room in those boats for both your father *and* your son! *(The patient now turns and checks out the intern.)* What about you, pal? Who cuts your hair?

Intern: I always go to Wally's Head Shed.

Patient: The next time you see Wally, tell him he's very creative. I've never seen a person with three parts in his hair before. *(A nurse enters with a blood pressure cuff. She is accompanied by an anesthesiologist. The patient then looks the nurse over. With a pleased expression.* Hey, fellas, looks like you've at least got some good entertainment here. *(Looks at nurse.)* Sister, you're a hands down favorite to win the contest.

Nurse: What contest?

Patient: Isn't there a Miss Piggy look-alike contest here today?

Creative Skits for Youth Groups

Intern: *(To surgeon.)* Doctor, it looks like the patient is going fast. We'd better put him under.

(The anesthesiologist places a mask over the patient's mouth and nose. The patient is not quite finished, however.)

Patient: *(Removes mask.)* Come on, doesn't this stuff come in strawberry?

(The anesthesiologist places the mask back over the patient's face. The patient then becomes motionless for the remainder of the skit. The nurse and anesthesiologist exit. The surgery room takes on a somewhat serious tone at this point.)

Intern: Doctor, if the patient is in critical condition shouldn't we do an exploratory first?

Surgeon: No, I've seen many cases similar to this one. I believe we can get right to the heart of the problem. *(The intern lifts his side of the sheet and surgery begins.)* We'll enter just above the appendix and make a jog at the gall bladder. *(Speaking as he operates.)* Then just before we get to the liver, we'll have a look. We should be arriving shortly.

Intern: Wait a minute, doctor. I think I caught a glimpse of something just after that left turn back there.

Surgeon: Ah, ha! This confirms my hunch. The patient has an acute case of criticulosis.

Intern: What exactly did you find?

Surgeon: *(Pulls saw out from under sheet.)* This is something we frequently find in more advanced cases of criticulosis. The patient is always cutting others down.

Intern: Do you think the problem is contained within the immediate vicinity?

Surgeon: Probably not. In fact, if you'll look closely, I believe you'll notice another malfunction.

Intern: I see what you mean. *(Pulls out book of matches.)* It appears to me that the patient is always out to burn others.

Surgeon: That's correct. And if I'm not mistaken, we'll discover another significant factor close by.

Intern: Right again, Doctor. Look over here. *(Pulls out inflated balloon.)* I'll have to admit, however, that I'm not sure what it is.

Surgeon: It's really not that difficult. Many patients with criticulosis have a severely inflated ego. *(Pops balloon.)*

Intern: I can understand that. But how does this problem right over here fit in? *(Pulls out dirty mirror.)*

Surgeon: That's related to the previous symptom. The patient's self-perception is grossly distorted.

Intern: You mean he can't see in himself what he sees in others?

Surgeon: Exactly. *(Wipes mirror off then places it back inside patient.)*

Intern: Doctor, do you think we've caught the problem in time?

Surgeon: I feel that we have corrected most of the difficulties. But just to be sure, let's look a little further. *(Peruses then pulls out hair pick.)*

Intern: What is it, Doctor?

Surgeon: It looks like just a small thing. But this patient has a well-ingrained habit of picking on others.

Intern: It seems to me that all of these disorders indicate a basic need for the patient to enhance his self-concept at the expense of others. As a matter of fact, *this* confirms it. *(Pulls out crutch.)*

Surgeon: Precisely. Criticizing others has obviously become a crutch for him.

Intern: Well, Doctor, if I'm not mistaken, we're about finished with the operation.

Surgeon: One would think so, but my experience has proven that there is one other area which sometimes harbors problems related to criticulosis. If you'll hang a left at the personality gland and continue the incision toward the patient's larynx, you may find that there is one last problem to correct. *(Intern continues incision toward the patient's feet.)*

Intern: Are we in the general vicinity, Doctor?

Surgeon: It's always been my experience that the larynx is in the "general vicinity" of the neck.

Intern: *(Embarrassed, moves toward neck.)* Oh, yes. Doctor, there's a pronounced irregularity in the patient's throat. I don't think I can diagnose it. *(Intern pulls out whip.)*

Surgeon: What we have here is evidence of the patient's propensity for lashing out at others.

Well, it appears to me that we've done everything we can for the patient. *(Surgeon and intern sew up the incision.)*

Intern: I'm curious to know something. Do you have any statistics showing the probability of criticulosis recurring?

Surgeon: Studies have shown that the patient's continued progress in recovering from criticulosis is largely dependent on his continuing a rehabilitation program. Generally speaking, if a patient faithfully follows this program, his or her chances of preventing a recurrence of the disease are good.

Intern: And just what is the key element in such a program?

Surgeon: *(With emphasis.)* Staying in touch with a Good Physician.

(A loud offstage voice is suddenly heard.)

Offstage Speaker 2: Hey, Nurse! I love your outfit. Do you do all of your shopping at the Salvation Army store?

(The surgeon and intern look at each other.)

Surgeon: It looks like it's going to be a long night. If I'm not mistaken, here comes another patient in *(Surgeon and intern look at each other and speak in unison.)* CRITICAL CONDITION!

Suggested Scripture

Matthew 7:1–5; Luke 6:31; Romans 14:13

3

Whatever Happened to Sin?

(or "Dragnet" Revisited)

We live in the age of the specialist. Your doctor may go by the title "family practitioner," and the man who picks up your garbage is a "sanitation engineer."

But what about sin? Has it, too, joined the age of specialization? Or has it simply become a master of disguise? In "Whatever Happened to Sin?" detectives Joe Friday and Bill Gannon take on the difficult assignment of trying to answer that question. You may be surprised at what they find!

Characters

Joe Friday (Joelle if played by a female)
Bill Gannon (Billy Jean if played by a female)
Captain
High school student
Old man or lady
Young boy
Policeman
Announcer

Props

Table
2 chairs
File folders
Portable stereo with headphones
Handcuffs
Telephone
Book
Test
Television set
Small notepad

This skit is written in the style of the old radio/television series "Dragnet." Friday is a dry, matter-of-fact character. He speaks in a monotone voice. Gannon, his partner, is also rather staid but speaks with a wry twist. The captain is just plain gruff!

Some of Friday's lines must be recorded onto a cassette tape. These lines are then played over the public address system at the appropriate times during the skit. (This creates the effect of Friday narrating the story himself.) Make sure there are no "clicks" when you play these tapes over the speaker system. There is nothing quite as distracting as electronic interference during a performance.

An important part of the skit is the theme song from the "Dragnet" series. This music can be incorporated wherever a dramatic bridge is necessary. The following single notes can be played on the piano to accomplish this: C, D, E-flat, C, then C, D, E-flat, C, F-sharp.

It would be helpful to watch an episode of "Dragnet" to get the feel of how the skit should go.

The detectives should be wearing trench coats whenever they are outside.

Announcer: *(In person.)* The story you are about to see is true. Well, almost. Only the names have been changed to protect the innocent. *(Exits.)*

(Theme music. Friday and Gannon are behind a table covered with shuffled papers.)

Recording 1: This is the city: Anytown, U.S.A. It was a hot, muggy July afternoon, the kind of afternoon you dream about in December. My name is Friday; my partner is Bill Gannon.

We were working Missing Persons that particular day. If there's any part of police work that's steeped in sheer frustration, its the attempt to find something that has simply disappeared. My partner and I were taking a break from the monotonous task of poring over police files when the captain walked in.

(The captain enters. Friday and Gannon are taking a leisurely break; Gannon has his feet propped up on the table.)

Captain: *(Gruff.)* Don't you guys have anything better to do than sit there and pretend to look busy?

Friday: *(Looks at Gannon.)* I suppose we could *stand* here and pretend to look busy. *(Both stand.)*

Captain: Very smart, wisenheimers. Listen, I've got a tough one here—never seen anything quite like it. Maybe by some slim chance, you *might* be able to help.

Gannon: We can try, Captain. What've you got?

Captain: Here's the file. *(Hands it to Gannon.)* I took the report a couple of days ago. It didn't really seem to fit misdemeanor or homicide, so I guess it's in *your* ball park now. But I have to admit one thing: It's not exactly a missing *person*.

Gannon: Well then, what is it, Captain?

Captain: *(Hesitant.)* You're going to find this hard to believe, but, well, it's *sin*.

Friday/ Gannon: *(They look at each other, then at the captain, then they speak in unison)* Sin?

Captain: *(Quickly, defensively.)* That's what I said—*sin!* I know, I know. It sounds crazy, but the guy who brought this in claims he's been trying to find sin for months now. He can't find it anywhere. He says he knows it's out there, but it's like trying to spot a chameleon.

Friday: What is it, Captain—plastic surgery?

Captain: *(Sarcastically.)* If I knew that, I wouldn't be here, would I? But I *don't* know, and we have to find an answer. Friday, Gannon, I'm putting you on this case. It won't be easy, but give it all you've got. Get out there and find out what happened to sin!

(Theme music. Friday and Gannon are going through file folders.)

Recording 2: It was Monday, July 16. The case would be a tough nut to crack, but we'd do our best.

The job began with the attempt to find names and possible suspects. We needed a lead, *any* lead. Before long, sixteen-hour workdays became standard operating procedure. Day after day went by, and still we had questions without answers. *(Friday and Gannon exit.)*

We knew sin was out there somewhere. We even had the creepy feeling that it was lurking around some corner, just waiting to leap out and taunt us, saying, "Catch me if you can!" But feelings don't stand up in court.

(Friday and Gannon re-enter.) Tuesday, July 24, 8:07 A.M. Gannon and I had been on the case for over a week now and had made virtually no progress. We were beginning to give in to the notion that the whole affair might be a hoax. That's when we got our first solid lead. It was a phone call. *(Friday picks up phone, pretends to talk.)*

The person on the other end had read about the case in the newspaper. She was an eyewitness to an unusual occurrence, and she figured it couldn't hurt to give us a call. It was a tip, and only a tip, but that was more than we'd had up till then. The location was the Thomas Jefferson High School at 42nd and Linwood. She thought she might have seen *(Pause.)* sin.

(Theme music. Friday and Gannon exit to car. Student enters from opposite side of stage.)

Recording 3: *(While driving.)* 8:25 A.M. Gannon and I were headed west on Highway 12. It wasn't long before we were at the Thomas Jefferson High School. Everything looked normal. We got out and went inside. We passed several students in the hallway. Nothing seemed out of the ordinary. Then we noticed one young man leaning against the wall and listening to an electronic music device. *(Stereo with headphones.)* He eyed us nervously. We made our approach.

(At this point, the student is into the music and pretends that he doesn't see the approaching officers. Gannon takes notes during each of the interviews.)

Friday: Excuse me. My name is Friday. This is Gannon. We'd like to ask you a few questions. *(No response from student. Friday lifts one side of the headphones up and shouts into the student's ear.)* Excuse me. We'd like to ask you a few questions.

Student: *(Acting surprised.)* Who, me?

Friday: Yeah, you. We're looking for something you might be able to help us find.

Student: If you're talkin' about Mickey Fuller's Springsteen album, I ain't seen it.

Friday: No, kid, that's not it. Where were you at 10:30 yesterday morning?

28 Creative Skits for Youth Groups

Student: *(Shifting nervously.)* Uh, kinda hot out today, isn't it?

Gannon: Just the facts, kid. What about yesterday morning?

Student: I was in school, right here.

Friday: In which room?

Student: Third floor, chemistry room. Hey, what's this all about, anyway?

Friday: What were you doing up there?

Student: Takin' a test.

Friday: *(Reaches over, pulls a test out of the student's book.)* This test?

Student: *(Cockily.)* Yeah. Not bad, huh?

Friday: Real good, kid. Do you always do this well in school?

Student: Maybe, maybe not.

Gannon: How about some straight answers?

Student: Okay, okay. So I'm not such a great student. *(Shamefaced.)* Fact is, I usually do terrible. But if I'm gonna graduate, I gotta pass this here test, see? So I get a little help from my friends.

Gannon: What friends?

Student: *(Boldly.)* Any friend I happen to be sittin' by—*That's* What friend!

Friday: You mean you cheat.

Student: *(Gaining confidence.)* Ha! Cheatin' went out with the hippies. This is called "creative learning," and everybody's doin' it.

Friday: Sounds like cheating to me.

Student: Get off it, man! If these clowns are gonna make a test hard enough for Einstein to flunk, you gotta do *something*. So I use my head. After all, isn't that what school's all about—to teach you how to get along in life? If you boys think that's "cheating," you're livin' in the past! *(Snatches test back.)*

(Theme music. Student exits. Friday and Gannon leave.)

Recording 4: *(While driving.)* 8:42 A.M. Gannon and I headed back. It was obvious we weren't going to find sin at the Thomas Jefferson High School. Oh, it fit the description all right, and there was little doubt in our minds that sin had been there at one time. But now nobody was talking.

Gannon: *(Still driving.)* I just don't get it, Joe. I really thought we had sin cornered back there. But just when we were ready to make the arrest, it turned out to be "creative learning." Sounds like an alias if you ask me.

Friday: Yeah. There was something all too familiar about what I saw back there. I may be wrong, but I'm beginning to think sin has become a master of disguise.

Gannon: I know what you—Hey, Joe!

Friday: What is it?

Gannon: I'm not sure, but look over there on the roof of that house. *(Pointing to a nearby rooftop.)* It's a hunch, and only a hunch, but I'm going to play it. Come on.

(They pull the car up, get out, and knock on the door of the house. After three successively louder knocks, an old man answers the door. The old man's part should be spoken with the appropriate inflections to indicate his age.)

Old Man: All right, all right, I'm comin'. *(Opens door.)* Wha'd 'ya want?

Gannon: My name is Gannon; this is Friday.

Old Man: No it ain't. This is Tuesday.

Friday: No, sir, Friday's my name.

Gannon: We'd like to ask you a few questions about that antenna up there on your roof.

Old Man: What's wrong with it? Is it too high or somethin'?

Friday: What's that antenna connected to?

Old Man: *(Sarcastically.)* To my wife. It's connected to my TV, wha'd'ya think it's connected to?

Friday: Mind if we have a look?

30   Creative Skits for Youth Groups

Old Man: At my wife?

Friday: No, at the TV.

Old Man: Help yourself. . . .

(They step in, and Gannon flips on the TV. They watch for a second and are astonished at what they see. Important: The timing and movements should be well thought out here. First, both Gannon and Friday look at the TV. Second, they look at each other. Third, they both look back at the TV. Last, they both turn and jump in front of the TV in an attempt to hide it.)

Gannon: *(Excitedly, and simultaneously jumping in front of TV.)* I knew it! Okay, buddy, we're placing you under arrest. *(Places handcuffs on the old man.)*

Old Man: Are you guys nuts? What are you arresting me for?

Friday: Harboring a fugitive. We found it, right here in your living room.

Old Man: You found what?

Friday/Gannon: *(In unison.)* Sin!

(Theme music, short.)

Old Man: You guys are off your rockers! You call a little skin and grit on the tube "sin"? Ha! *That,* my friend, is "fine art." Don't you guys know what the real world is all about? *(Begins to look off in the distance, as if drawing a picture in his mind.)* The human body is beautiful. *(Scolding.)* And you guys oughta be ashamed of yourselves for treating it like it's something dirty. Where's your sense of decency? Maybe *you* don't have a taste for the finer things in life, but that doesn't mean *all* of us are living in the Dark Ages! Now, until your attitude changes, I'll thank you to get these things off of my hands!

(Theme music. Gannon takes the cuffs off. The old man exits. Friday and Gannon leave in the opposite direction.)

Recording 5: Sin had eluded our grasp once more. But by now, Gannon and I knew that it was just a matter of time before we began nailing down some hard facts. It would be a tough job to break down the well-calculated alibis we'd been running into. But it wouldn't be too tough, for two tough cops.

Wednesday, August 1, 8:07 P.M. Things were beginning to

happen. Slowly the pieces of the giant puzzle were falling into place.

(Friday and Gannon are back at headquarters. The captain enters.)

Captain: *(Upset.)* Do you mean to sit there and tell me you could've put the pinch on sin *twice*, and you came back empty-handed?

Friday: *(Looks at Gannon.)* I suppose we could *stand* here *(both stand)* and tell you. . . .

Captain: *(Interrupting.)* Knock it off, wisenheimers. What happened?

Friday: Captain, we're sure we saw sin at least twice. But trying to gain a positive identification on it is nearly impossible. Nobody will admit they've had anything to do with it.

Captain: What's your story, Gannon?

Gannon: Frankly, I'm baffled by the whole thing, Captain. To be honest with you, I'm beginning to think a person could be looking sin right between the eyes and not even recognize it.

Captain: So where do we go from. . . . *(Phone rings and interrupts. The captain storms out.)*

Friday: *(Answers phone.)* Missing persons; this is Friday. *(Pause.)* Yes, ma'am, I know what day of the week it is. Friday's my name. What can I do for you? *(Pause.)* Uh-huh. I see. *(Pause.)* Uh-huh. Thank you. *(Hangs phone up.)*

Gannon: What is it, Joe?

Friday: *(Stands to leave.)* Get the cuffs. The lady says she just saw sin do a number.

(Theme music, short.)

Recording 6: *(Gannon and Friday are driving.)* 8:22 P.M. We headed south on Interstate 5 and took the Harbor Boulevard off-ramp. It wasn't long before we spotted the location the lady had described. It was an amusement park called Dizzyland. The police officer on the scene briefed us on what had taken place. The incident had occurred by the ride called the Cosmic Crusher. The suspect was in custody. Now it was *our* turn. *(Policeman leaves.)*

Friday: *(To young boy.)* My name is Friday; this is Gannon. We've got a report here that says you cut into this line, right in front of a nine-year-old child. Is that right?

Boy: *(Wearing T-shirt and cutoffs.)* Oh, my mom is gonna die when she finds out about this. No! *I'm* gonna die when she finds out about this!

Friday: Just the facts. Did you take a cut in this line?

Boy: I suppose you could say I took a cut, but I wouldn't say that.

Friday: What would *you* say happened?

Boy: Now, let's see. What did my teacher call that again? Oh, yeah. "Positive aggression"—that's what it is—"positive aggression."

Friday: Sounds to me like you bumped a little kid out of line.

Boy: No, you've got it all wrong. It's "positive aggression," purely p-sychological *(pronounces hard p first, uncertain of pronunciation).* See this ride here, the Cosmic Crusher? It closes up in just a little while. I've only been on it six times today. I won't be able to come back here until next week, maybe even longer. So you can see, if I'm gonna get my last ride in, I gotta exercise my rights.

Gannon: What about the kid you bumped out of line?

Boy: Aw, c'mon. He probably lives around here someplace. His dad might even own this joint for all I know. And besides, who's more important—him, or me?

Friday: *(Quickly.)* That's it. Gannon, book him on a three sixty-two.

Boy: *(While being handcuffed.)* Hey, wait a minute! What are you doing? What's this "three sixty-two" all about?

Friday: You're going for a ride after all. Get in the car.

Boy: But what are you taking me in for?

Friday: We're booking you on a charge of total self-centeredness. You might even call it sin.

(Short theme music as they finish handcuffing him.)

Whatever Happened to Sin?

Boy: *(Just before entering car.)* Hey! What about Jimmy Johnson? He did the same thing just yesterday!

Friday: But Jimmy Johnson didn't get caught—yet.

(Theme music.)

(They drive to headquarters, where an "interrogation" takes place. This is all occurring visually while the narration is playing.)

Recording 7: 8:55 P.M. We moved back toward headquarters. We'd finally caught sin red-handed. But something the kid had said stuck with me. What *about* Jimmy Johnson? Could there be more to sin than we had originally thought? Could there be an accomplice?

9:12 P.M. Back at headquarters we questioned the suspect, and after a lengthy interrogation, we broke him. He admitted that he was involved in a world-wide organization known as a sindicate. It seemed everyone he knew was involved to some degree. Many of them had apparently been unwittingly sucked into it before they even knew what was happening.

9:25 P.M. We obtained arrest warrants for the suspects we had questioned earlier. Their real names turned out to be Cheating and Lust. They were apprehended within the hour.

10:35 P.M. Gannon and I called it a day. We knew in our guts that this wasn't the last we'd ever see of sin. It would be a long time before we knew the whole story. But at least for now, this chapter was finished.

(Theme music, dramatic. At this point, all three suspects form a line and face the audience with a shameful look.)

Recording 8 (Announcer): On August 27, 1986, the suspects named Cheating, alias Creative Learning; Lust, alias Fine Art; and Self-centeredness, alias Positive Aggression; were placed on trial in Superior Court. In a moment, the results of that trial.

(Short theme music.)

Recording 9 (Announcer): After a brief trial, the suspects Cheating, Lust, and Self-centeredness were found guilty of attempting to hide their true character. Dabbling in sin carries a maximum penalty of death in the state of Unforgiveness, and was therefore recommended by the jury. However *(suspects exit, leaving the stage empty)*, due to an unusual circumstance, the sentence was dropped when another Man offered to die in their behalf.

The only name given for the Man was *(slight pause for emphasis)* "a Friend of sinners."

(Theme music.)

Suggested Scripture

Genesis 4:7; Romans 5:12–15;
1 Timothy 5:24; 1 John 1:8–10

4
Long Distance

Good friends are hard to come by. That's why it's so important to stay in touch with the people we care about. "Long Distance" is aimed at giving you and your audience the incentive to "reach out and touch" someone who has drifted out of your life.

Characters

Buzz Jackson, disc jockey
Jerry Roberts, youth minister
Airline stewardess
2 airplane passengers
Announcer (offstage)

Props

8 chairs (arranged to simulate airplane interior)
Tray
Drinks, including 1 can of beer, 1 can of 7-Up, and 1 can of root beer
Luggage

The skit opens with all the passengers aboard except Jerry, who is just boarding. Important: The front row of seats must have only two chairs in it. Buzz is seated in one, and Jerry will eventually sit in the other.

Stewardess: *(Pointing toward empty seat.)* You'll find seat A-17 right over there, sir.

Jerry: Thank you. Great, a window seat! *(Sits down.)*

Announcer: Ladies and gentlemen, please prepare for takeoff by fastening your seat belts and extinguishing all smoking materials at this time. Thank you.

(All the passengers cooperate. To portray the takeoff, all should lean on the back legs of their chairs simultaneously, then level off. This is both humorous and effective.)

Announcer: Thank you for your cooperation. Please feel free to move about the cabin as necessary until further notice. Enjoy your flight.

Jerry: *(Rising.)* Speaking of necessities. . . . *(He begins to walk toward restroom, then spots Buzz. There is a slight pause; the two then begin a high school chant in unison.)*

> Who potato, who potato,
> Half-past alligator,
> Riff ram bowligator,
> Sis! Boom! Bah!
> Roosevelt High School,
> Rah! Rah! Rah!

(The two slap hands on the final "rah," almost hitting a nearby passenger.)

Jerry: Phil, is it really you? What's it been—almost ten years now? How are you? *(Sits down in the empty seat directly across the aisle from Buzz.)*

Buzz: It's me, all right, and I'm doing great. I *thought* I recognized that old Jerry Roberts walk, but after ten years I wasn't quite sure!

Jerry: I suppose it *is* a one of a kind. But I still can't believe it's *you!* *(Jokingly reaches over and pulls on Buzz's hair.)* Hey, is it still all yours?

38   **Creative Skits for Youth Groups**

Buzz: *(Laughs.)* So far. But forget about that. What about you? Have you gone and done anything drastic, like getting married?

Jerry: As a matter of fact, I did. We're heading for the big number four anniversary next month. How 'bout you, Phil? As I recall, you and Susie Ballinger were quite the item our senior year.

Buzz: I guess we were at that. But it just didn't seem to work out. I'm still single.

(At this point, both Buzz and Jerry pick up their chairs and move a couple of feet in opposite directions. This is to visually indicate the distance that's come between them. There is a brief silence, and then the conversation continues.)

Jerry: So, Phil, what are you doing in Chicago?

Buzz: Business. I had a convention over at the O'Hare Inn.

Jerry: Oh, really? What business are you in?

Buzz: Have you ever heard this before? *(In fast-talking DJ's voice.)* "Put the pedal to the metal 'cause we're goin' uptown, just you and the Buzz'll be countin' em down. Welcome to the Buzz Jackson Super 40 Survey!"

Jerry: You mean, *you're* Buzz Jackson?

Buzz: One and the same.

Jerry: How did that ever happen? You must be one of the hottest commodities in the country right now!

Buzz: Oh, you know how it goes. You catch a few breaks here and meet the right people there. Somehow, in between, you climb the ladder. I guess life's been pretty good to me. But what about you? The way you used to ace old Nickerson's accounting tests, you're probably headed for an H & R Block takeover by now!

Jerry: I guess I did okay on most of those tests. But as it turned out, something came along that interested me more.

Buzz: What could be more interesting than keeping track of money?

Jerry: Kids.

Buzz: Oh, really? How many kids *do* you have?

Long Distance 39

Jerry: The last I knew, about thirty-five.

Buzz: *(Shocked.)* Jerry! And I thought disc jockeys were into records!

Jerry: *(Quickly.)* Oh, no. I'm talking about the kids at my church. You see, I'm a youth pastor.

Buzz: *(Surprised and softly.)* You're a youth pastor!

(Jerry and Buzz again move their chairs apart another couple of feet and continue the conversation after a short silence.)

Jerry: So, Phil, er, I mean Buzz. Do you still have the ol' '63 Plymouth? Man, could she make Ronnie Newman's Chevy look wimpy!

Buzz: I hate to have to break the news to you, but I laid her to rest two years ago.

Jerry: *(Puts hand over heart.)* I hope you gave her a decent farewell.

Buzz: Sure did. I kicked her in the rear fender. But in my sorrow I went down to the local Ford dealer and drove home a new conversion van. If you thought the '63 Plymouth was a hot machine, you should see this beauty! Compact disc player, air conditioning, and a built-in bar— *(Buzz stops mid-sentence and remembers that Jerry is a pastor. He immediately attempts to rectify his statement.)*—bargain seats. Yes, sir, I got a real bargain all right. Head rests, arm rests, and the seats even recline. It was a real deal!

Jerry: Wow! A van would sure be perfect for our youth group. We do a lot of things on weekends like visiting shut-ins and helping out at the soup kitchen. As far as I'm concerned, weekends were made for ministry. But a van would come in handy for driving our basketball team around, too. Squeezing five six-footers into a Chevette gets a little uncomfortable. Of course, you'd know all about that. You always were the star point guard on our church team.

Buzz: I guess I was pretty active in our youth group. *(Pauses.)* But broadcasting keeps me hopping these days. You know, meetings, production, and all that. I will have to admit that it would feel kind of good to shoot a little hoop again. But I probably couldn't hit an outside shot anymore if my life depended on it. Yeah, I guess you get your kicks from kids, and I get my highs spinning hits.

(Buzz and Jerry move their chairs apart again. After a brief silence, the conversation continues once more. A stewardess enters carrying a tray of refreshments.)

Stewardess: *(To Buzz.)* Would you care for anything to drink, sir?

Buzz: Sure, I'll have a beer. *(Glancing at Jerry.)* Uh, a *root* beer, that is.

Stewardess: *(To Jerry.)* And you, sir?

Jerry: I'll have a 7-Up. *(Takes a drink then looks at Buzz.)* You're thinking about it, too, aren't you?

Buzz: The high school cafeteria?

Jerry: Yep. I still can't believe you put castor oil in the juice machine.

Buzz: *(Laughing.)* Yeah. That was the smoothest drink Roosevelt High ever served up!

Jerry: Harold Walton kept wondering why his sandwich was sliding down so fast!

Buzz: Those were the days, weren't they? By the way, Jerry, you never told me what *you* were doing in Chicago.

Jerry: Actually, I'm just passing through. I've been in New York at a youth workers' seminar. I would like to have stayed for the last day, but I have the sermon this week, and I need to put some time into it. Speaking of sermons, what church do you go to now?

Buzz: *(Uncomfortable.)* Well, uh, just this last Easter I went and checked out the church down the street from where I live. Great acoustics in there. I don't exactly remember the name of the preacher. I *do* remember the sermon lasted too long, though. In fact, if it lasts that long next year, I may be forced to stop going to church on a regular basis.

(Buzz and Jerry again move apart, followed by another brief silence. The skit then resumes.)

Announcer: Ladies and gentlemen, we'll be landing in Denver shortly. Please fasten your seat belts and extinguish all smoking materials at this time.

(Everyone fastens their seat belts, and the plane lands. Have everyone on board the plane lean forward together and then all "bump" on the runway at the same time. The other two passengers exit, then Buzz unfastens his seat belt and removes his carry-on luggage from the overhead storage compartment.)

Buzz: *(Still from opposite side of where Jerry is.)* Well, Jer, this is where I change planes. It's been great seeing you. Best of luck in the preaching business. You know, we shouldn't let the distance come between us.

Jerry: You're right, Buzz. Take care of yourself.

(Here, still separated, Jerry extends his hand toward Buzz, and the two share a parting "handshake." They move their hands up and down in handshake fashion. It is yet another visual portrayal of the distance that has come between them. Buzz then heads off the plane, and just before exiting, he speaks.)

Buzz: Hey, Jer. *(Buzz points at Jerry and begins their high school cheer. Jerry joins in, but the cheer has lost its meaning.)* Who potato, who potato. . . . *(They stop, and Buzz exits. Jerry is still sitting, looking where Buzz was just standing. The stewardess enters again.)*

Stewardess: *(Spotting Jerry.)* Excuse me, sir. Is anything wrong? If you don't mind my saying so, you look like you just lost your best friend.

Jerry: *(Looks at her, then speaks.)* Not if I can help it. *(He quickly grabs his bag and heads for the exit.)* Hey Buzz, wait up!

Suggested Scripture

1 Samuel 18:1–4; Proverbs 17:17;
John 15:13

5
Change-O-Rama

Wouldn't it be great to be somebody you've always wanted to be? Perhaps. But maybe after doing some shopping at Change-O-Rama, you'll discover that you're satisfied just being yourself!

Characters

Mr. Turner

Salesclerk

Steve

4 teenage girls

Props

For the "woodsman" look:
 flannel shirt
 hiking boots
 suspenders
 blue jeans
 work gloves

For the "scholar" look:
 white shirt
 tie
 dress slacks
 calculator on belt
 pencil behind ear
 books under arm
 black-rimmed glasses

For the "athletic" look:
 sweatshirt
 jogging pants
 tennis shoes
 sweatband
 tennis rack

Play money

2 hard hats

Pair of white gloves with fingers cut off

The setting is a store called Change-O-Rama.

Salesclerk: Where would you like me to put these hard hats, Mr. Turner?

Turner: Put them over there next to the nail aprons. The construction look is really in this season.

Salesclerk: And what about these Michael Jackson gloves?

Turner: Those can go to the back of the store for now. We'll have a close-out special on them next week.

(The focus shifts to a customer about to enter the store.)

Steve: Boy, oh, boy! Lana really came through for me this time. She says the blind date she has me set up with is a real knockout. Well, I'm going to make sure she isn't disappointed.

(Steve enters the store.)

Salesclerk: Welcome to Change-O-Rama. What can we do for you today?

Steve: I saw your ad on Channel 38 a couple of nights ago. I have a blind date tonight, and well, I just don't want her to be disappointed. You know what I mean?

Turner: Pal, you came to the right place! The experts here at Change-O-Rama have been changing people for the better for over twenty-five days now.

Steve: But can you guarantee that my date will like me when I leave here?

Turner: Friend, when you walk out of here, you'll be a different person.

Steve: Do you really mean it?

Salesclerk: That's why we're here. Like our motto says: "A buck will change your luck!" *(Holds out hand.)*

Steve: Only a buck? *(Reaches into wallet.)* Wow, how can I go wrong? *(Hands dollar bill to salesclerk.)*

Turner: That's the spirit! Now, what would you like to try first? This week's special is the Trapper John, M.D., look. Wanna give it a shot?

Steve: Hmmm. No, I don't think so. A bald head would make my nose look like a cucumber. Do you have anything a little more outdoorsy?

Turner: Outdoorsy? You want outdoorsy? Have we got outdoorsy!

(Salesclerk goes to the rear of the store and brings back the "woodsman" costume on hangers.)

Salesclerk: Paul Bunyan, eat your heart out!

Turner: *(Takes shirt off hanger, holds it out to Steve.)* Shall we? *(Steve puts clothes on over his current attire. The salesclerk and the owner are talking while Steve is changing.)* Is that him, or is that him?

Salesclerk: That's him, boss.

Steve: Do you really think so? It *does* feel kind of natural.

Turner: Well, don't take *our* word for it. You've already paid your buck; get out there and change your luck!

Salesclerk: And right now is your chance. Look. *(Points to girls coming down sidewalk.)*

Steve: Hey, all right! Thanks a lot, you guys. I'll be sure and tell all my friends about this place.

(Steve leaves. The scene shifts to the sidewalk. Girls 1 and 2 are strolling by, and Steve approaches them.)

Girl 1: *(To friend.)* Oh, I know what you mean! Phil is *so* intellectual! I understand he's going to be able to attend college entirely on scholarships. I don't know about you, but I just adore a man with that kind of intelligence!

(Steve stops, looks at his clothes, then heads back to Change-O-Rama.)

Turner: Welcome to—Oh, it's you again! Don't tell me. One of them fainted the minute she saw you, and you rushed back here for an oxygen mask. Happens all the time.

Steve: Well, no, not exactly. Listen, I've been thinking. The outdoors look just isn't me. After all, I graduated from the eighth grade, and well, maybe I should go with something a little more scholarly than just your average run-of-the-mill woodsman.

Turner: It's up to you, pal. We'll do our best to make you look intelligent. But considering what we have to work with, we'll have to charge you extra.

Salesclerk: It's like our motto says: "Slip us a five, and your brain'll come alive!" *(Laughs and holds out hand. Steve pays up.)*

Turner: *(To salesclerk.)* Go get Albert Einstein here his outfit, would you? *(The salesclerk leaves and reappears with the scholar clothes and paraphernalia. Steve puts the new outfit on over the previous one.)* You know, I hate to admit it, but I believe you're right. It's definitely you. I don't know why we didn't think of it before. The books, the pencil, the calculator—it all adds up.

Salesclerk: A Harvard man if I ever saw one.

Steve: *(Proudly.)* In that case, gentlemen, I bid you farewell.

(Turner and the salesclerk look at each other, then shake hands. Steve heads out of the store. The girls are strolling by again from the opposite direction.)

Girl 2: But in the final set of the mixed doubles he was just totally awesome. Poor Dave started ducking every time Rob served! Can you imagine how Heather must've felt being Dave's partner! I'm just glad I was on Rob's side! I'm going to ask him to help me with my backhand. He's *so* athletic!

(The girls leave. Steve looks at his clothes again and then heads back to Change-O-Rama.)

Turner: It's you again. Your brain waves were too much for her, right? Just put one of those hard hats over there on. That'll keep the radiation down.

Steve: No, in fact, I should've used my head to begin with. Take a good look at my build.

Turner: Do I have to?

Steve: Yeah. Now come on. What do I remind you of? *(Begins making sweeping gestures as if playing tennis.)*

Salesclerk: A pecan.

Turner: *(To salesclerk.)* A pecan is a nut. *(The salesclerk and Turner look at each other, then at Steve.)* Now that you mention it . . . .

Creative Skits for Youth Groups

Steve: *(Interrupts.)* No, no. Think! Racket, net, court. . . .

Turner: Oh, I've got it. You were caught illegally importing butterfly nets, and they're taking you to court.

Steve: No! I'm a tennis player! Look at the natural grace of my swing. *(Does movement.)*

Turner: What you're trying to tell us is that you want to try a little more "athletic" look.

Steve: Right! Can you guys fix me up?

Salesclerk: No problem! You know what our motto is: "Hand us a ten, and you won't be back again!"

Steve: *(Reaching into pocket again.)* I sure hope you're right.

(The salesclerk goes and brings back the athletic clothes.)

Salesclerk: Here we are, Ace.

Turner: *(Helping Steve put new clothing on top of the rest.)* Now, are you *sure* this is what you *really* want to be?

Steve: Hey, do I look like a person who can't make up his own mind? This is definitely me, and if I don't know who me is, I don't know who does!

Turner: All right, all right. Maybe you *do* have a little feisty streak in you! As a matter of fact, this athletic look may be just the change you needed. Go get 'em, tiger!

Steve: GRRRRRRR!

(Steve exits. Girls 3 and 4 are walking by this time. Steve begins doing the sweeping tennis gestures.)

Girl 3: *(To girl 4.)* Well, aren't *you* getting brave these days. A blind date no less. What did Lana say the guy's name was?

Girl 4: I think she said his name was Steve. But I guess I'll find out for sure tonight.

Steve: *(Startled.)* Excuse me, did I hear you say "Lana"? And "Steve"?

Girl 4: And just who are you, might I ask?

Steve: Well, this is quite a coincidence! I'm Steve.

Change-O-Rama

Girl 4: Oh, right. And I'm Princess Diana.

Steve: I don't think you quite understand. I'm Lana's friend Steve. You must be my date for tonight.

Girl 4: Nice try, Mr. Cool, but I'm not into phony tennis players. Now if you'll excuse me. . . .

Steve: No, really. I'm Steve. See?

(Steve tries to peel off the first of his outfits. He immediately hits part of the scholar layer.)

Girl 4: Don't tell me. On the days you're not playing the pro tennis circuit you're a nuclear physicist. Why don't you make like a backpacker instead and take a hike?

Steve: *(Panicking, he hits the woodsman layer.)* You don't understand! I'm really just an ordinary guy underneath all this stuff! Can't you tell?

Girl 4: Look, *Steve,* I don't know who you really are, but if you're trying to score with me, you're definitely striking out. So long, Mighty Casey. *(The girls leave.)*

Steve: But, but. . . . Oh, why me?

(Just as Steve is whimpering, the salesclerk comes along.)

Salesclerk: Hey, what's this? Don't tell me the "athletic" look didn't do the trick.

Steve: *(Upset.)* Listen, mister, I've had it up to here with all this changing. I'm going back to being who I was intended to be—me! Pretending to be somebody else is costing me too much. And speaking of costing too much. . . .

Salesclerk: Whoa there! Lighten up, pal. You know, I've been doing some thinking about your situation. What you need is some good one-liners to get the ladies on your side. Yes sir, the more I think about it, you're a perfect candidate for the comedian look. And you know what our motto is: "A twenty'll make you funny!" *(Holds out hand.)*

Steve: Thanks, but no thanks. It's an interesting pose, but you can keep your clothes. I'm just going to be me, *(Gives salesclerk a*

48   Creative Skits for Youth Groups

disapproving look.) 'cause *I* come for free! *(Steve exits, salesclerk scratches head and then heads off in the opposite direction.)*

Suggested Scripture

Genesis 1:26–27; Hebrews 2:7;
1 Peter 3:3–4

6
Patent Approved

In Matthew 5:14, Jesus says we are to be "the light of the world." Sometimes it's hard to believe that our light makes much of a difference. But in a world where there's so much darkness, even the faintest glimmer can help to show someone the way.

"Patent Approved" takes a lighthearted look at our tendency to underestimate the value of an individual witness, or light.

Characters

Will Grant, patent approver
Dee Klein, assistant to the approver
Everett Ready, entrepreneur

Props

- A wheel cover mounted on a square piece of plywood
- A rope looped through four bricks, then tied
- A 12" x 36" poster board, covered on one side by aluminum foil. The letter *A* should be written about halfway down on one edge of the covered side, with the letter *B* opposite. A large arrow should then be drawn under each letter, pointing to its counterpart on the opposite edge of the poster board.
- Flashlight
- A gerbil "maze" or an assembled *Mousetrap* game
- A rubber hand stamp
- 4 tags (can be 4 x 6 index cards, to be attached to the individual inventions)
- Sheet of paper
- Two visors

Shoe box

A desk

Three chairs

A sign reading "Patent Office"

Note: A critical factor in the success of this skit is to have it in an area that can be totally darkened at the appropriate time.

The skit begins with Will Grant and Dee Klein ready to face another day in the U.S. Patent Office. Both should be wearing visors.

Klein: I can't tell you how grateful I am to be working under someone with your experience, Mr. Grant.

Grant: It's taken a long time, but I do feel qualified to determine what new ideas merit our stamp of approval, Miss Klein.

Klein: *(Looking at table covered with inventions.)* And it looks like we have plenty of candidates for your expert evaluation this week.

Grant: Yes, it does appear that we have a full schedule ahead of us. We might as well get started.

(Miss Klein picks up the wheel cover secured to the piece of plywood.)

Klein: First we have a Mr. Roland Hubbs who seems to have reinvented the wheel. He calls his version the "Puncture-Proof Wood Ply Wheel."

Grant: I never tire of this kind of ingenuity. How does it work?

Klein: *(Reads from attached tag.)* "This wheel, because of its unique design, eliminates the possibility of tire blowout. An added feature is that the wear is distributed evenly on all four sides."

Grant: Hmm, that *is* a new angle. Detroit will thank us for this one. *(Stamps the tag.)* Patent approved! What's next, Miss Klein?

Klein: *(Picks up foil-covered poster board.)* This one comes from a Marian Stout. She calls it the "EverThin Figure Enhancer."

Grant: This could be a big breakthrough. Read on.

Klein: *(Reading from tag.)* "The 'EverThin Figure Enhancer' is the easiest way ever to look fit and trim. Simply hold the mirror at arm's length and bend arrow A in toward arrow B until desired figure is achieved. (Miss Klein demonstrates.) It's the surest way ever to stay forever thin."

Grant: It doesn't take much reflection to see that Miss Stout's invention will ring up hefty sales come next Christmas. *(Stamps the tag.)* Patent approved!

You know, Miss Klein, today's crop of inventions seems to be particularly useful. Let's hurry on to the next one.

Patent Approved 53

Klein: *(Goes to gerbil maze.)* A Mr. Fuzzy Hunter submitted this device. Unless I miss my guess, he's attempted to build a better mousetrap.

Grant: It does seem to be an interesting device. On what premise does it operate?

Klein: Mr. Hunter calls his invention the "Humane Maze Mouse Trap." *(Reading from tag.)* "This is the trap designed with the house mouse in mind. Simply place the bait of your choice in the inner chamber of the unit. When the mouse detects the scent of food, he or she will be led into the maze. Whereas other mousetraps would ruthlessly quash the life out of the defenseless creature, the 'Humane Maze Mouse Trap' simply drives the little fellow or gal to sheer exhaustion. At this point, most mice choose to slumber peacefully. This affords the homeowner the opportunity to carry the harmless rodent to a remote area for release into its natural habitat. Not only does this preserve the life of the animal, but also provides it valuable cardiovascular exercise prior to the rest period."

Grant: Amazing! It won't be long before the world will be beating a path to Mr. Hunter's doorstep. *(Stamps tag.)* Patent approved! Well, Miss Klein, it looks like we're moving along quite nicely. It's hard to believe so many wonderful inventions would pass through our hands on one day alone.

Klein: *(Picking up rope-connected bricks.)* Believe it or not, thanks to a Mrs. Shirley Down I think the best may be yet to come.

Grant: Oh, really? What has Mrs. Down come up with?

Klein: It's called the "Stay-Put Skirt Weight." *(Reading from tag.)* "Finally, a practical solution to an age-old problem. The Stay-Put Skirt Weight can be sewn directly into the hemline, or simply tied on to the exterior and worn as a fashionable designer accent. *(Grant attempts to demonstrate.)* Either way, this item will put an end to those frightfully embarrassing moments so often encountered by ladies on breezy autumn days."

Grant: Now there's a down-to-earth approach if I've ever seen one. *(Stamps tag.)* Patent approved!

Klein: It's surprising how many creative people there are out there with helpful ideas, isn't it, Mr. Grant?

Grant: Yes, but we mustn't be too hasty. Just because someone thinks he or she has a clever idea doesn't automatically mean that it's going to be approved. As I've told so many would-be inventors in the past, "You won't make many dollars from something that doesn't make any sense."

Klein: *(Chuckles.)* Well said, Mr. Grant.

(Knock on door.)

Grant: Ah! ha! It sounds as if we have a potential seeker of success knocking on our door of opportunity.

(Miss Klein opens the door, Everett enters.)

Everett: Hello. My name is Everett Ready. I'd like to speak with someone about getting a patent.

Klein: You came to the right place. My name is Dee Klein, and this is the head patent approver, Will Grant.

Grant: *(Shakes Everett's hand.)* Nice to meet you, son. Now, just what is it you'd like to get approved for a patent? Of course, I should tell you that we're a mighty fussy bunch around here, so don't be disappointed if your idea doesn't make the grade. But, of course, everyone gets a fair shake. So, what new and useful item do you have for us?

Everett: *(Hands Grant a sheet of paper.)* This paper describes my product. But I've discovered the best way for people to understand it is to show it to them. *(Pulls flashlight out from box.)* I call it "The Light."

Grant: Very interesting. Pay attention here, Miss Klein. This may be a good opportunity for you to learn something. At first glance, the device appears to be just an ordinary flashlight. But nobody would be stupid enough to try and patent such a simple thing as that. Obviously, it must do something more than just shine. My guess is that it beeps when you whistle at just the right pitch. That way, it's impossible to lose. Am I correct?

Everett: No, I'm afraid not.

Klein: I think *I* may have it, Mr. Grant. Judging by the small size of the bulb and the large batteries the unit requires, I believe there may be a calculator mounted somewhere on the handle.

(Mr. Grant peruses the flashlight.)

Grant: A valiant attempt, Miss Klein, but I'm afraid your observations just don't add up. I'll have to admit, though, I'm in the dark on this one myself. Just what *does* this item do that makes it so special, Mr. Ready?

Everett: As far as I know, it simply shines.

Grant: No offense, but your idea doesn't hold a candle to your competitors'. I'm afraid you're not going to get very rich trying to market something as ordinary as a flashlight.

Everett: I'm not concerned about getting rich. In fact, I'll be glad to share my light with anyone who needs it.

Grant: That's admirable, but there's another slight problem. The flashlight was already patented years ago. I ought to know. I stamped that little item myself.

Everett: *(Holding flashlight, and pointing to the handle.)* Oh, I'm not interested in getting your approval on *this* part. *(Turns the flashlight on and points to the actual beam.)* This is what I'd like to get patented.

(The next three lines are said in rapid succession.)

Klein: That's light!

Everett: That's right!

Grant: That's not too bright! Why in the world would you want to patent that?

Everett: I've discovered that many people don't realize just how valuable light can be. By getting it patented, I figure folks will be naturally curious to know what's so special about it. Then, when they come and ask me about it, I'll do my best to "enlighten" them. (Turns flashlight off.)

Grant: Maybe you can enlighten *me* as to what you're talking about.

Everett: Gladly. I first got the idea when somebody shared *their* light with *me*. All of a sudden I could see much more clearly. Before, when I walked in the dark, I used to stumble over things. Sometimes I'd find myself heading in the opposite direction I wanted to go. Why, once on a campout, I even led a whole group of my friends down the wrong trail. When I saw the same trail in the light, I was surprised how dangerous it really was. That's when I decided to show as many people as I could the true value of light.

Klein: If you ask me, it sounds like a publicity stunt just to get people to take a look at what you have to offer.

Everett: I'm not sure I'd call helping others to see more clearly a "publicity stunt." But I'll have to admit I am anxious to get The Word out.

Grant: Well, Mr. Ready, I'm sorry, but, I don't think it will be possible to accommodate your "brilliant" idea. I'm sure Miss Klein will concur with my decision. *(Klein nods approval.)* I *will*, however, give you a litle bit of advice. The next time you try to obtain a patent, make sure it's for something people can really use. Never insult the public by trying to market a commodity, *(Points to flashlight, chuckles, shakes head.)* such as light, that there's simply no need for.

*(At this point, **all** of the house lights should be turned off **at the same time.**)*

Klein: Looks like accounting forgot to pay the electric bill again, Mr. Grant.

(At this point, Grant and Klein fumble around for the flashlight. Klein then flips it on and aims it at the descriptive sheet on the desk.)

Grant: *(Clears throat, then picks up rubber stamp.)* But then, heh-heh, we were wrong about the Wright Brothers, too. *(Stamps tag.)* PATENT APPROVED!

(Flashlight is then turned off.)

Suggested Scripture

Psalm 119:105, Matthew 5:14–16, John 3:19–21, Ephesians 5:13, 14

7

A Quaint Little Custom

A Live "Slide" Show on Appreciation

Here's a creative and inexpensive way to produce an entertaining slide show on the theme of appreciation. But you won't be using slides. Instead, you'll be using people!

Characters

- Narrator
- Mike Mercer
- Mr. Mercer
- Mrs. Mercer
- Mrs. Drew, convenience store clerk

Props

- Poster board
- Blow dryer
- Vacuum cleaner
- Picture frame
- Aluminum foil
- Steering wheel
- Hose with attached spray-gun type nozzle
- Snow cone cup (can be an equivalent)
- Cardboard box
- Juice cooler/slush cone machine (must have a spout). The slush cone machine can be made by putting the juice cooler inside of a cardboard box and allowing the spout to stick through a hole cut in its side. Mark the box in large letters: SLUSH CONES.

This is how it works: The room should be as dark as possible. The show should proceed as if there were actual slides in the projector. As the narrator reads the script, the participants will form the scene being described directly in front of the screen. At the appropriate time, the projector (still empty) will flash on, giving the effect of a slide being shown. After the "slide" has been viewed, the projector light will be taken away while the actors/actresses prepare for the next scene.

You will need a slide projector that you can make perfectly dark for a few seconds between each "slide." If all you have is a carousel-type, use a piece of cardboard to cover up the lens between each scene change. The participants will have to be fast, and they will have to stand still while the "slide" is being shown. After all, it is a slide show, *not a movie!*

Narrator: Welcome to Union Center, Maine. *(Slide 1.)*

(Slide 1: A sign, possibly on poster board, that reads, "Welcome to Union Center, a Fine Place to Live." The holder can kneel in front of the screen and hold the sign up so that the sign and his/her arms are the only things showing on the screen.)

Narrator: Union Center is the home of the 1973 Class F state basketball champs, the Maple Leaf Quality Motel, and Smiley's Friendly Gasoline and Convenience Center. *(Slide out.)*

Union Center is also the home of one Rodney W. Mercer, your almost basic Maine kid. *(Slide 2.)*

(Slide 2: Rodney should stand in front of the screen holding a picture frame around his face.)

Narrator: As you can see from this yearbook photo, Rodney Mercer is the picture of innocence. *(Slide out.)*

One morning Rodney was getting ready for school. Now Rodney usually styled his hair each day using an Acme blow dryer. *(Slide 3.)*

(Slide 3: Rodney with blow dryer up to head.) (Slide out.)

Narrator: As he was standing there with his blow dryer, he began to think. *(Slide 4.)*

(Slide 4: Rodney changes position, now resting chin in hand, looking at blow dryer.)

Narrator: He thought about how funny his hair would look if he didn't have that little gadget. People would probably think he'd plugged his *finger* instead of his blow dryer into the outlet! *(Slide out.)*

Realizing he'd been taking the blow dryer for granted all this time, he gave it a little pat on the nozzle. *(Slide 5.)*

(Slide 5: Rodney smiling at blow dryer and patting it on its nozzle.)

Narrator: It was his quaint little way of saying thanks. *(Slide out.)*

After Rodney had finished doing his hair, he wandered downstairs and found his mother doing the vacuuming. *(Slide 6.)*

(Slide 6: Mrs. Mercer with a vacuum cleaner and attached hose.)

Narrator: Rodney, being the neat and tidy individual that he was, *(Slide out.)* decided to compliment his mother on a fine job. *(Slide 7.)*

(Slide 7: Rodney talking to his mother.)

Narrator: He said, "Boy, Mom, you sure have done a nice job with the vacuuming. And so fast, too. For a minute I thought I was going to have to—er, I mean, be able to help you finish. But I see you're almost done." *(Slide out.)*

Narrator: Mrs. Mercer thanked Rodney for his willingness to help and then reminded him that keeping the floors clean hadn't always been that easy. *(Slide 8.)*

(Slide 8: Mrs. Mercer talking to Rodney.)

Narrator: "Rodney," she said, "it used to take your grandmother a long time to get the housework done. But we're more fortunate. Thanks to some smart person, we have a much easier way to keep our house clean than she did." *(Slide out.)*

Then she added, "You know, Rodney, sometimes I take our little vacuum cleaner for granted, but I surely do appreciate how much easier it makes my housework, especially when I have to vacuum someone's popcorn out of the sofa." Then she reached over and gave the vacuum cleaner hose a little pat on the nozzle. *(Slide 9.)*

(Slide 9: Mrs. Mercer holding vacuum cleaner hose, patting the end of it.)

Narrator: It was her quaint little way of saying thanks. *(Slide out.)*

By now it was time for Rodney to head off to school. His dad usually dropped him off, so the two said goodbye to Mrs. Mercer,

(Slide 10: Rodney with school books in one hand, waving goodbye with the other. Rodney's dad is beside him, also waving goodbye.)

Narrator: walked out the door, and hopped into the car. *(Slide out.)* As the two were driving along *(Slide 11.)*,

(Slide 11: Rodney beside his dad, both looking straight ahead. Mr. Mercer should have a steering wheel in his hands.)

Narrator: Mr. Mercer happened to glance down at the fuel gauge. *(Slide out.)* Both he and Rodney were surprised to see that they were almost out of gas. *(Slide 12.)*

(Slide 12: Same position. Mr. Mercer is now pointing to the fuel gauge. Rodney sees it also, and both have surprised looks on their faces.)

Narrator: "Rodney," Mr. Mercer said, We need to stop at Smiley's Friendly Gas Station and Convenience Center and fill 'er up." *(Slide out.)* So they did.

As Mr. Mercer was filling the tank, he began thinking how nice it was to have a car to ride to work in. Then he looked at the gas hose in his hand and thought of something he appreciated even more. *(Slide 13.)*

(Slide 13: Mr. Mercer with gas hose in hand, speaking to Rodney.)

Narrator: "You know, son," he began, "I'm thankful we have a nice car to drive. But without gasoline to put in the tank, we sure wouldn't get very far!" *(Slide out.)*

And with that, Mr. Mercer gave the gasoline hose a little pat on the nozzle. *(Slide 14.)*

(Slide 14: Mr. Mercer patting the gasoline hose on the nozzle.)

Narrator: It was his quaint little way of saying thanks. *(Slide out.)*

It was still early in the day, but Rodney had a lot to ponder. He'd never really stopped to think about all the things he just took for granted. Things like blow dryers and vacuum cleaners and even gasoline.

Mr. Mercer finished filling the tank. Then he and Rodney went inside to pay. Rodney liked going into Smiley's Friendly Gasoline and Convenience Center. The main reason was because the clerk, Mrs. Drew *(Slide 15.)*,

(Slide 15: A nice shot of a smiling Mrs. Drew.)

Narrator: was very nice to Rodney and his father. She always seemed to have a smile on her face and something friendly to say. *(Slide out.)* It was right about then that something struck Rodney like a bolt of lightning. *(Slide 16.)*

(Slide 16: Someone should hold a tinfoil-covered "lightning bolt" over Rodney's head. Slide out.)

Narrator: All morning he'd been thinking about the *things* he'd been taking for granted. But what about the *people* he took for granted? Wasn't Mrs. Drew more important than a blow dryer or a vacuum cleaner or a tankful of gas? He decided right then to say something. *(Slide 17.)*

(Slide 17: Rodney speaking to Mrs. Drew, Mr. Mercer listening in.)

Narrator: "Mrs. Drew," Rodney started, "I would like you to know how much I appreciate the way you treat us when we come in here. You always seem to have a smile on your face and something friendly to say." *(Slide out.)*

Mrs. Drew was surprised but very glad that Rodney had spoken up. "Why, thank you, Rodney," she told him. *(Slide 18.)*

(Slide 18: Mrs. Drew with her arm around Rodney in a gesture of thanks.)

Narrator: "I always look forward to seeing both of you, too." She had a special little twinkle in her eye that made Rodney feel good. *(Slide out.)*

Then she continued. "I'll have to be honest with you, though. I'm not quite my usual smiling self today. You see, our slush cone machine is broken down *(Slide 19.)*

(Slide 19: Mrs. Drew pointing to an empty snow cone cup.)

Narrator: and I just hate to see the children come in here only to be disappointed. *(Slide out.)*

They all just stood there for a moment. Rodney began to think about all the slush cones that machine had made over the years. He also thought about how it was just taken for granted *until* it was broken. All of a sudden, he realized what must be wrong with it. He pulled Mrs. Drew over and whispered something in her ear. *(Slide 20.)*

(Slide 20: Rodney whispering to Mrs. Drew.)

Narrator: With that *(Slide out)*, Rodney and his father walked out and got in the car. As they were driving away, both of them looked back at Smiley's Friendly Gasoline and Convenience Center. Sure enough, Mrs. Drew was taking Rodney's advice. *(Slide 21.)*

(Slide 21: Mrs. Drew patting the slush cone machine on the nozzle.)

Narrator: She was giving the slush cone machine a friendly pat on its nozzle. It was just her quaint little way of saying thanks. *(Slide out.)*

Suggested Scripture

Psalm 136:1; Luke 17:11–19; John 6:11; Ephesians 5:20

8
Sin-ema

"Sin-ema" takes a behind-the-scenes look at the way some movies are produced. Is what you're seeing really what you're getting?

Characters

Movie director
His/her subconscious mind

Props

Clipboard for director
Cassette player for background music

The setting is a movie screening where a director is explaining to the audience the finer points of film production.

The movie can be imaginary, but an option is to do it in silhouette. This can be done by hanging a white bedsheet up and shining a slide projector on it from behind. All actions are then done behind the screen and appear to the audience in silhouette. (The romantic scene can be treated with humor and still be effective.) Another option is to do the movie portion as a second skit within the main one.

An important stage effect is to have the subconscious mind stand immediately behind the director. At the appropriate times, the subconscious mind will step out from behind the director.

Director: *(Addressing audience.)* It is with a great deal of pleasure that I welcome you to the initial screening of the movie *Credit Risk*. Your attendance here tonight shows that you have a genuine interest in the technical and artistic aspects of quality film production.

I'd like to thank the executive producer, Mr. Steven Spillmore, and all the others who contributed to the production of this film. Without further ado, why don't we turn down the lights and enjoy the premiere showing of *Credit Risk*.

(The lights are turned down, and soft movie music begins. The director is explaining as the movie rolls.)

Director: Many of you seasoned theater-goers undoubtedly know that the plot of *Credit Risk* centers around a young man's unsuccessful attempt to obtain a department store charge card. At first, one would question whether an entire movie surrounding such a theme could effectively command one's attention for over two hours. But that is the beauty of the theater. Under the tutelage of a master director, what appears to be nothing more than another thin plot suddenly becomes a thought-provoking study in interpersonal relationships.

(The director freezes his action; the subconscious mind then steps out from behind him and speaks to the audience.)

Subconscious: I'm sure glad you people don't know what I'm *actually* thinking. I mean about what my movies are *really* saying to you. Take, for example, what I just said about thin plots being turned into "thought-provoking studies." Come on. Do you really buy that? *(Sarcastically.)* I don't care if you want to see a movie about New York City garbage collectors. As far as I'm concerned, if you've got the cash, I'll find the trash.

(The subconscious mind steps back behind the director, who in turn unfreezes and continues.)

Director: As we move along, we find the star, Murphy Edwards, entering a department store in Chicago's Loop area. Edwards, or Brent, as he goes by in the film, has just finished filling out his charge card application. It's at this point in the production that some of the most intense realism ever portrayed on the screen occurs. Brent approaches the young woman behind the credit counter. But, as you can see, his application is being turned down. In a fit of emotional rage, he lashes out at the woman. As I've said regarding some of my previous films, the most powerful display of realism in film production is the four-letter word. Here, in *Credit Risk*, you're hearing what is, in my opinion, the finest possible verbal abuse.

(The director again freezes; his subconscious mind steps out from behind and speaks.)

Subconscious: What I'm really trying to say is that since you're too "pure" to use filthy language, I'll do it for you. *(Sarcastically again.)* Eventually, after you've heard enough dirty words, you won't even notice them. Who knows? Eventually you might even want to try some of them out yourself.

(The subconscious mind steps back behind the director. The director unfreezes, and once again the movie review continues.)

Director: As the drama continues, Brent becomes enraged at the thought of being unable to buy a compact disc player on credit. Feeling justified in his actions, he pulls a .38 caliber pistol from his jacket and impulsively pulls the trigger. I should like to point out that as the director of this film, I felt that to edit this particular portion of the movie would compromise my integrity as a professional. Therefore, viewers are able to experience the inevitable gruesome results. It is not a pleasant sight to endure, but a realistic one. Indeed, *reality* is the key element here. The dead victim, by the way, will be starring in my next film, *Rocky 27*.

(Here the director again freezes his action; the subconscious mind steps up to address the audience.)

Subconscious: What you actually have here is a banquet to satisfy your appetite for violence. *That's* the "reality" of the situation. If you really wanted to experience the pain of someone who's hurting, all you'd have to do would be to go see my neighbors.

Sin-ema

They know all about it. Their son was just killed by a drunk driver. Too bad *that* wasn't just a movie.

(The subconscious mind again steps behind the director, and the movie rolls on.)

Director: As you can see, Brent flees the scene of the crime. In a state of panic, he hails a taxi. Unknown to him, riding in the vehicle which stops is a brunette fashion model. Sensing that he needs a friend, she begins a conversation with him. She invites him home, still oblivious to his previous actions. At this point in the film, we chose to allow the story to develop naturally. The romantic scenes are explicit, yet tastefully done. Their impact on the emotions can leave little doubt as to their intrinsic importance to the overall plot.

(The director freezes, the subconscious mind takes the spotlight and once again speaks to the audience.)

Subconscious: Let me put it another way. Sex sells. The local social services director isn't buying that though. She's seen too many emotionally destroyed pregnant teenagers walk through her front door to believe that Hollywood doesn't play a role in real life. Oh, I know, I know. You're saying to yourselves, "It's *them* doing it, not me. And besides, it's only a movie. That makes it okay." But does it really?

(The subconscious returns to its previous position, and the director continues his evaluation.)

Director: It's always difficult to know how to end such a stirring presentation as *Credit Risk*. We do feel, however, that our treatment of the closing scenes in this film are something you'll rarely encounter in the film industry. You'll notice that as the film draws to a close, Brent, now regretting his actions, is reading the Bible in his remote hideaway cabin located in the Yukon Territory. I would at this point like to explain how this ending originated. As many of you know, I became a born-again Christian in 1977. Or was it 1967 when I became a born-again Christian? I don't quite remember. At any rate, throughout the entire film I have attempted to integrate the principles by which I live. Therefore, it seemed particularly appropriate to write the ending of the movie to parallel my own personal spiritual pilgrimage.

(Director freezes for the last time; the subconscious mind comes front and center.)

Subconscious: "Spiritual pilgrimage" is *one* way to put it. Actually, it's just plain good business. Let's face it. There are a lot of you out there whose consciences get a little uneasy in the theater. Well, it wouldn't bother you half as much if I could convince you that what you're looking at came from the mind of a church-going man. That way you might be able to persuade yourself that it's all right. Who said you can't have your cake and eat it too? It sure wasn't anybody at Silver Screen Studios.

(The subconscious mind heads back behind; the director unfreezes and gives his final remarks.)

Director: And there you have it, friends, the premiere of what I hope will become a classic, *Credit Risk,* starring Murphy Edwards. I hope this experience has been not merely entertaining, but also educational. As one of Hollywood's movie directors, I've always felt that a behind-the-scenes look at film production is the best way to make the viewer aware of what's really happening, both *on* the screen and *off*. Thanks for coming, and don't forget to tell your friends what you've learned here this evening. Good night!

Suggested Scripture

Psalm 119:37; Philippians 4:8;
2 Timothy 2:22

9
Backstabbers

Gossip is a lot like a forest fire. It's easy to get it started but difficult to put it out.

"Backstabbers" is a humorous yet painfully true look at gossiping and backbiting. Watch a taping of this TV game show and see if you think anybody really comes out a winner.

Characters

Johnny, studio announcer
Bill Baxter, game show host
Fred, contestant
Virgil, contestant
Gabrielle, contestant
Wally, participant
Janitor
Cue card holder
Optional: Model

Props

3 cue cards:
  APPLAUSE
  MOAN
  GO, GO, GO!

Hand-held microphone

1 pair of headphones

Back-stab-o-meter
  This can be made from a piece of poster board. It should be in the form of a clock, with the numbers 1–100 placed around the perimeter. A needle is not really necessary since the scoring is imaginary. A more elaborate version could be made with a needle which is controlled from behind.

Backstabbers 71

Optional:
    Cordless telephone
    Box of throat lozenges
    Crock pot

The stage is arranged like a television game show studio. The contestants should be sitting in the audience.

Johnny: *(From one side of the stage.)* And here's your host on "Backstabbers," Bill Baxter!

(Bill comes out; the cue card holder prompts the audience with the applause card.)

Bill: Thank you, and welcome to another "Backstabbers" show. As you know, backstabbing can be fun, and the great thing about it is that anybody can do it! We hope you at home will play along with us. For those of you who've never seen the game, here's how it works: Each contestant will have the opportunity to backstab our computer-selected participant. The backstabs will be registered electronically on our Back-stab-o-meter. The contestant with the highest score at the end of the game is the winner. It's that simple! So sit back and get ready for some of the juiciest gossip this side of the Mississippi!

Our computer-selected participant has been sitting backstage, unable to hear the studio activity. As always, the participant selected has never seen the game played before. In other words, he or she is completely innocent! Isn't that great?

All right then, with that out of the way, let's get set to play another rip-roaring round of "Backstabbers"! *(The applause card is held up.)* Johnny, why don't you tell us who our first contestant is?

Johnny: Bill, our first contestant on "Backstabbers" is a 34-year-old used-car salesman from Badmouth, Illinois. Meet Fred McNertny!

(Applause card. Fred walks in wearing bright, gaudy clothes.)

Bill: Welcome to "Backstabbers," Fred.

Fred: Thanks a lot, Bill. I'd just like to say how much the wife and I have enjoyed your show over the years. We have the home version of the game, and somebody in the house is always playing it. In fact, it's kind of a family tradition with us to come home from church every week and play a few rounds over lunch.

Bill: That's fantastic! "Backstabbers" is truly a game you can play anytime and anywhere. But as they say, "On with the show!"

(Escorts Fred to his position on the stage.) Johnny, who's our next contestant?

Johnny: Our next contestant is Gabrielle Valenti, a suburban housewife from Buffalo, New York. Gabrielle, come on down!

(Applause card is held up. Gabrielle excitedly steps on stage.)

Bill: Welcome to our show, Gabrielle.

Gabrielle: *(Out of breath.)* Oh, thank you, Bill. Just call me Gabby. Everyone else does.

Bill: Fine, Gabby. Now if you'll just step over next to Fred, we'll meet our last contestant. Johnny?

Johnny: Bill, our last contestant comes to us all the way from Grande Boca, California. He's a lawyer, and he enjoys public speaking. Ladies and gentlemen, let's welcome Mr. Virgil Slanderson!

(Applause card. Virgil enters.)

Bill: And a hearty Hollywood hello to you, Virgil!

Virgil: It's great to be here, Bill. I just hope I do all right.

Bill: Have you ever won anything before?

Virgil: Well, let's see—there was *Brown vs. the State of Ohio* back in '81, and then—

Bill: *(Interrupts.)* Oh, that's right. Well, with your being a lawyer and all, I suppose you're hoping for a "case" of good fortune.

Virgil: Yes, I suppose you could say that.

Bill: Then why don't you take your place next to our other contestants, and we'll be all set to play the game!

(Virgil takes his position.)

Bill: And here's the moment we've all been waiting for. It's time to meet our computer-selected participant. Johnny, who's the lucky person?

Johnny: Bill, the person we'll be backstabbing today on the show hails all the way from Dubuque, Iowa. He's a certified public accountant and is unmarried. Ladies and gentlemen, welcome our participant, Mr. Walter Magillicutty!

(Applause card goes up, and a rather common looking and slightly overweight gentleman comes out from behind the stage. He is wearing a white shirt, bow tie, and suspenders.)

Bill: Walter, welcome to our show. Do you go by Walter or Wally?

Wally: Wally will be fine.

Bill: Okay, Wally. Now, I understand you've never seen "Backstabbers" before. Is that right?

Wally: That's true. I'm afraid I'm not familiar with this program.

Bill: No need to feel bad about it, Wally. First-timers *always* seem to make the best participants here on "Backstabbers." Don't they audience?

(Applause card.)

Wally: I hope I play the game the way I'm supposed to.

Bill: I'm sure you'll do just fine. Ladies and gentlemen, it's time to take Wally over to our sound-proof booth, so-o-o.... *(Bill escorts Wally to an imaginary sound-proof booth. He opens the door, and Wally steps in. Bill places the headphones on Wally, then steps out and locks the door. He picks up a microphone.)* Wally, can you hear me? Are you comfortable? *(Wally nods yes.)* Wally, we're going to turn off the microphone now so you won't be able to hear what's being said about you. Just make yourself at home, relax, and enjoy playing the game. I know *we* will! *(Sound in booth is now off.)* Friends, Wally can't hear us now, and that's just the way it will remain throughout the entire game. *(Bill looks at contestants.)* Now you all know how we play the game. Right? *(All nod.)* Of course many of our regular viewers know that this is a special week here on "Backstabbers." It's Anything Goes Week, and that's just what we mean—*anything* goes! Speaking of that, if you're all set, why don't *we* get going! *(Applause card is raised.)* Fred, are you ready to play the game?

Fred: I think so, Bill.

Bill: Then what are we waiting for? Fred, backstab!

Fred: Bill, believe it or not, I heard that Wally doesn't go to church every week!

(The other two contestants gasp and shake their heads. In the booth, Wally slowly grabs his lower back and grimaces in slight pain. He doesn't know what is happening, but he knows that he is hurting.)

Fred: And what's worse—

Bill: *(Cutting Fred off.)* Oh, I'm sorry, Fred, but we can only accept one answer. But it was a good one. Faulty church attendance is a new stab here on the show. Let's see how you did. *(They all turn toward the Back-stab-o-meter.)* Back-stab-o-meter sa-a-ys 29!

(Moan card is held up to the studio audience. At this point a janitor comes onto the stage and speaks to Bill.)

Janitor: Excuse me, but I think that fellow over in that there booth is feelin' a might uncomfortable. Maybe you should check on him.

Bill: *(Talking out corner of mouth.)* Mister *(or Sister)*, we're on national television. Would you get off of this stage? *(The janitor reluctantly leaves.)* Well, Fred, it's not the highest score we've ever had on "Backstabbers," but who knows? Let's move over to Gabby. Are you nervous, Gabby?

Gabby: Oh, I've got a few butterflies in my stomach, but I'll be okay.

Bill: Then if you're ready, so are we. Gabby, backstab!

Gabby: Looking over the brief life sketch we were given on Wally, it seemed to me that he became a certified public accountant at a very young age. I'm willing to go as far as to say that Walter Magillicutty *cheated* in order to pass his C.P.A. exam!

(Applause card is held up. The other contestants gasp, etc. Wally, in the booth, grabs his lower back again. He is experiencing a sharp pain and much discomfort. He still is not sure what is going on.)

Bill: Wow, what a whopper! But there's only one way to tell if Gabby's score will match or surpass Fred's. Let's have a look. *(All turn toward the Back-stab-o-meter.)* Back-stab-o-meter sa-a-ays 74! Congratulations, Gabby! You're our new leader!

Janitor: *(Rushing on stage again.)* Excuse me, sir, but I think that fellow is really hurting in there. Cain't you do somethin' about it?

Bill: *(Agitated and off-mike.)* Listen, pal, if you don't get off of this stage, *you're* gonna be hurting. Now beat it!

(The janitor slowly leaves, glancing back at Wally in the booth.)

Bill: Yes, Sir, that was quite a stab. But the game's not over yet! Virgil, do you think you've got enough ammunition to win it all?

Virgil: *(Confidently.)* I'm loaded.

Bill: I like your style. But style alone won't necessarily win the big one. So, Virgil Slanderson, backstab!

Virgil: *(Sarcastically.)* Mrs. Valenti obviously didn't do her homework very well. But I dug beneath the surface and came up with a great big scoop of dirt. By combining the life sketch with the weight of the participant, I came to an obviously logical conclusion. I think it's quite reasonable to assume that this man has been eating much heartier than the average accountant in Dubuque, Iowa, should be. This, in turn, leads me to believe that, during the course of his experience as a C.P.A., the participant would have had to embezzle at least fifty thousand dollars in order to support this habit. *(Turns to Wally.)* Take that, you gluttonous crook!

(The applause card is held up, and the contestants gasp, etc. Wally, still in the booth, now feels intense pain in his lower back. He grimaces and begins to buckle under the pressure.)

Bill: How about *that* one, folks? Have you ever heard a juicier piece than that? Let's see just how juicy our Back-stab-o-meter thinks it is! *(All turn toward Back-stab-o-meter.)* 10, 20, 40 *(Go, Go, Go card is held up; cue card holder should "cheerlead" audience.)* 70, 73, 74! You've tied Gabby Valenti's score! But wait— *(Bill looks over at booth; Wally finally drops lifeless to the floor.)* It looks like we have a winner! And we also have an all-time high score here on "Backstabbers"—a perfect 100! Congratulations, Virgil. *You* are our new champion backstabber!

(Applause card is raised. The janitor rushes on stage again.)

Janitor: Listen, you bonehead, cain't you see that guy's about half dead? I don't know what this is all about, but I'm callin' an ambulance. I shore hope it ain't too late! *(Looks at Wally lying prone on floor, then rushes off to use the phone.)*

Bill: Well, Johnny, why don't you tell our new champion just exactly what he's won?

If desired, as the prizes are being listed, a model can bring each item out to display.)

Johnny: *(Still offstage.)* I'll be glad to. First of all, from AB&C Telecommunications, a cordless phone system! *(Applause.)* From now on, your gossip will never be more than an arm's length away! Second, we have a one-year supply of Can't Stop Talkin' throat lozenges! *(Applause.)* Just throw one of these little gems down the 'ol trap door and keep on yapping! Last, but not least, from Terra-Firma Earthenware, your very own crock pot! *(Applause.)* Just plug this beautiful unit into any standard electrical outlet, and you'll always have a potful ready! Bill?

Bill: Friends, that's all the time we have today on "Backstabbers." We hope you'll be able to join us again next time. And remember to send for the home edition of our game. Like I always say, "When it comes to gossip, there's no place like home!"

So long everybody! See you again soon on "Backstabbers"!

Suggested Scripture

Psalm 15:1–3; Proverbs 17:9; John 7:24

10
The Health Nuts

For a lot of people, there's nothing quite as appetizing as a Twinkie and a can of pop. But lately more and more people are realizing the benefits of a healthy lifestyle.

Being health conscious doesn't necessarily mean one has to eat lentil pie for dessert. That's for health "nuts." But some people, such as the Pendletons, are health "nuts" in their own unique way.

Undoubtedly you'll have a lot of fun performing this skit. But remember: No eating between lines!

Characters

Julie Pendleton, high school student
Mrs. Pendleton
Mr. Pendleton
Sally Collins, Julie's best friend

Props

Sweet rolls
Box of granola
Box of sugar-sweetened cereal
2 bottles of Coke
A table with 3 chairs
A few empty pop bottles and a jar of honey, on table
Lunch sack
Sugar bowl and spoon
Coffee cup

The skit opens with the Pendleton family gathering for breakfast. Mr. P enters wearing a jogging outfit. Mrs. Pendleton, her hair in curlers and wearing a bathrobe, speaks to him.

Mrs. P: Good morning, dear. I'm glad to see that you're taking your new fitness program seriously.

Mr. P: Yes. You know, I've developed a whole new outlook on life since I started wearing these clothes. So, what's for breakfast, sugar?

Mrs. P: Sweet rolls, honey.

Mr. P: Oh, good! I hope you used whole-wheat flour in them. It's much healthier, you know.

(Julie enters dressed for school.)

Julie: Good morning, everyone!

Mr. P: Hello, babycakes.

Mrs. P: Hi, sweetie pie. Are you hungry?

Julie: Oh, didn't I tell you? I've decided to follow my health teacher's advice and cleanse my system by just drinking liquids. Could you get me the bottle of Coke from the fridge? *(To dad, drinking coffee.)* By the way, Pop, do you think you should be drinking so much coffee? It's just loaded with caffeine.

Mr. P: I suppose you're right. Sugar, would you get me a bottle of Coke?

(Mrs. P hands the drink to her husband then pours herself a bowlful of (clearly marked) sugar-sweetened cereal. She then proceeds to heap several spoonfuls of sugar on top of it.)

Mrs. P: Well, *I* think the secret to good health is found in nuts and grains. That's why I always sprinkle a little granola on my food. *(Sprinkles a dab of granola on her cereal.)*

(Knock on door.)

Mr. P: I'll get it. I need to break these new sneakers in. *(He goes to answer the door. Sally enters.)* Well, if it isn't our favorite little cupcake! How are you this morning, Sally?

Sally: I'm just fine, Mr. P. *(To Julie.)* I just thought I'd stop and see if you needed a ride to school, Julie.

Julie: Thanks anyway, Sally, but I'm trying to get a little more aerobic exercise. I think I'll walk across the street to the bus stop instead of riding with you.

Sally: Why don't you just walk *all* the way to school?

Julie: Oh, I'd have to work up to something like that. It's almost two blocks away! *(The phone rings. To parents.)* I'll answer it. You two need to conserve your energy. *(Answering phone.)* Hello, this is Julie speaking. *(Pause.)* Oh, hi, Ralph. Tonight? Well, I'd like to, but I really should start getting to bed at a decent hour. A person can think much more clearly when she's had a good night's sleep. Besides, I have to stay up all night cramming for my health test. Maybe next time, okay? All right. Bye. *(Hangs up phone.)*

Mrs. P: You girls had better get going. And don't forget your lunch, sweetie pie. *(Hands lunch to Julie.)* I put some chocolate-covered granola bars in it. I don't want you eating the junk food they serve in those vending machines at school.

Julie: You're a sweetheart, Mom. See ya when I get home.

(Both girls leave.)

Mr. P: Well, I guess I'd better go get dressed for work.

Mrs. P: Aren't you going jogging?

Mr. P: I don't think that would be a good idea. The exercise book I'm reading says you're not supposed to do any vigorous activity for at least two hours after you eat. By that time, I'll be at work. Speaking of which, I'd better run along. *(He leaves.)*

Mrs. P: Well, my efforts have finally paid off. I would never have dreamed that my little gumdrop and her sugar daddy would be so concerned about fitness. At last, I've turned my whole family into health nuts!

Suggested Scripture

Ecclesiastes 10:17; Daniel 1:8–20;
1 Corinthians 3:16-17; 6:20

The Health Nuts

11
The Blind Optometrist

It's easy to place confidence in someone who has all the right credentials. But, unfortunately, sometimes the people we *do* choose to trust are in no better shape than ourselves!

Once Jesus used the illustration of a blind person leading another blind individual, and described the less-than-desirable results. After a visit to "the blind optometrist," you'll see quite clearly what he meant!

Characters

Owen Bundy, high school student
Optometrist
Patient
Receptionist
Teacher
Gwen, student
Harold, student
2 or 3 other students (All students can double as passengers.)
Bus driver

Props

Doctor's attire
Blood-pressure cuff
Tongue depressor
Chairs
Telephone
Clipboard
Steering wheel

Scene 1

(A classroom.)

Teacher: *(Pointing to blackboard.)* And what is the answer to this, Gwendolyn?

Gwen: The square root of 121 is 11.

Teacher: Very good, Gwendolyn! Now, Harold, how about this one? *(Points to blackboard again.)*

Harold: 63 divided by three is 21.

Teacher: Excellent, Harold. Now this last one should be easy. Owen, why don't you give it a try?

Owen: *(Squinting at blackboard):* Uh, seventy-seven?

Teacher: Owen! You should know by now that two plus two is four! *(The bell rings.)* All right, class. Now don't forget about the quiz tomorrow. Owen, I'd like to see you for a moment. *(The class disperses, and Owen approaches the teacher.)* Owen, you seem to be having difficulty with your math lately.

Owen: Well, to be honest with you, I've been having some trouble seeing recently. As a matter of fact, I couldn't even tell where the blackboard was on that last problem.

Teacher: Maybe you'd better see an optometrist.

Owen: Teacher, I'm not sure I could *see* an optometrist if I had to. But just the same, I have to agree with you. I'd better make an appointment right away. In fact, I'll use the telephone out in the hallway.

Teacher: Well, just be careful crossing the street when you go home.

Owen: Teach, I'm in high school! I'll be fine.

(Owen turns to leave and stumbles over a chair. He then turns and sheepishly waves goodbye to his teacher.)

Scene 2

(The school hallway. Owen feebly makes his way down the hall, looking for the telephone. He finds one and dials.)

Owen: *(Pauses.)* Yes, this is Owen Bundy, and I'd like to see the optometrist. Could you schedule an appointment for me? *(Pauses.)* Well, yeah, this afternoon would be great, but how can you get me in so fast? *(Pauses again.)* Oh. Well, all right. I'll be there at four o'clock. *(Owen hangs up the phone and talks to himself again.)* How about that! This is sure my lucky day. And they say you can't get good service anymore! I'd better go catch the bus right now if I'm going to be there on time. *(Owen rushes out to catch the bus.)*

Scene 3

(Owen arrives at the bus stop but has trouble telling which is the right bus to take. His head follows the passing traffic, and again he talks to himself.)

Owen: Boy, I sure hope I get the right bus. They don't paint very big street names on them these days. Hey, that looks like it there. Let's see. *(Squinting.)* Dodge Avenue. I think that's close to where the optometrist's office is. *(Steps out to flag it down; vehicle rushes by, nearly hitting Owen.)* Whew, wrong Dodge. That was a close one. I'm just glad the optometrist's office isn't on Peterbilt Street! *(Pointing.)* That must be the right bus coming now.

(The bus stops. Note: The "bus" is portrayed by arranging passengers as they would be on an actual bus, some reading newspapers, etc. The driver of the bus should be steering with an actual steering wheel or a substitute. The passengers then walk behind him, remaining in their respective positions as they move. Owen boards the bus, and it "drives" around the audience once to give the effect of distance. The bus then stops, and Owen steps off.)

Owen: Ah, here it is. *(Glances at watch.)* I guess I am a few minutes late. But there'll probably be a long wait anyway. *(Owen enters the optometrist's office. Another patient, an older man, is in the waiting room. Owen looks at the patient.)* What are you in for?

Patient: Mistook my pastor's head for a honeydew melon. The wife said that was the last straw. So I came to get the ol' sights adjusted. What about you?

Owen: I thought two plus two equaled seventy-seven.

Patient:	That's bad.
Receptionist:	Are you Owen Bundy?
Owen:	That's me, all right.
Receptionist:	Come with me, please.
Owen:	Really? I can't believe I'm getting in this fast!

(The receptionist leads Owen to an exam room and has him sit down.)

Receptionist:	The doctor will be with you in a few moments. *(The receptionist exits.)*
Owen:	Talk about speedy service! This doctor must really know what he's doing.

(Shortly thereafter a tap, tap, tap is heard outside the room. The doctor enters, wearing sunglasses and using a red-tipped white cane.)

Doctor:	Well now, ma'am, what can I do for you today?
Owen:	*(In state of shock.)* Well, uh—
Doctor:	I can tell right now that you're in the wrong place, ma'am. You need a throat specialist.
Owen:	Uh, I'm not exactly a "ma'am."
Doctor:	Oh, sorry. I guess I should've looked before I leaped, so to speak. *(Chuckles.)* So, what seems to be the problem?
Owen:	*(Still hesitant.)* I've been having some trouble with my eyesight lately.
Doctor:	I see. In that case, we'll need to run a few preliminary tests. *(Fumbles around in pocket and takes out a tongue depressor.)* All right, now open your mouth and say "Ahhhhh."
Owen:	*(Confused.)* Ahhhhh.
Doctor:	*(Looks in Owen's ear.)* Your throat's in great shape. Let's have a look at your ears. *(Looks in Owen's mouth, which is hanging open.)* Hmmm. It appears to me like you could stand to use a few Q-Tips.

Owen: But, but—

Doctor: Just one last thing. If you'll roll up your sleeve we'll run a check on the ol' pumper power. *(Doctor somehow retrieves blood pressure cuff then places it around Owen's head, just above his ears. Caution: If you are using the real thing, be careful!)* Wow, you must be a weight lifter, huh? *(Doctor gives the pump a couple of squeezes. Owen panics.)*

Owen: *(Tearing cuff off head.)* Look, Doc, I can see one thing perfectly clear. You're in no better shape than I am! *(Runs from room toward waiting area, followed closely by doctor with tapping cane.)*

Doctor: Somebody stop that man! He can hardly see! He might hurt himself!

(Owen exits, and as the doctor nears the waiting room, the other patient, spotting the doctor, runs after Owen.)

Receptionist: *(Looking down at her clipboard.)* Well, there goes another one. But then, a case of the blind leading the blind will do it every time.

Suggested Scripture

Psalm 146:8; Matthew 23:16–24; Luke 6:39–42

12
The Factory

People need people, yet we often let our differences keep us from reaching out to others.

Today there is worldwide strife because people of various backgrounds do not see eye-to-eye. But if we could trace our lineages, our discoveries might make a difference in the way we treat each other. Join the Pinkertons, Vince Brown, and the Redford family as they embark on a most unusual journey in search of the Factory.

Characters

Roving narrator

Alex Pinkerton, retired millionaire

Martha Pinkerton, civic leader

Vince Brown, sales representative

Curtis Redford, coal miner

Wilma Redford, housewife

Billie Lee Redford, their ten-year-old daughter

Factory foreman

T.V. announcer

Props

4 3-inch pink construction paper circles

2 3-inch brown construction paper circles

6 3-inch red construction paper circles

The construction paper circles should be placed on the cheeks of each person accordingly: pink—the Pinkertons; brown—Vince Brown; red—the Redfords. The circles can be attached with double-sided adhesive tape or an appropriate substitute. These circles stay on the cheeks until the time indicated in the script.

The Factory 89

Monopoly game
Card table
Radio
Easy chair (for Vince Brown)
Plant
End table
Tomato sandwich
Chair (for Alex Pinkerton)
White lab coat
Trace Your Factory Kits
   4 manila envelopes
   Pencils
   Several sheets of paper
   3 regular envelopes

Cardboard box big enough to house a person. One side of the box will be cut in the shape of a TV screen. A live TV announcer will be hidden inside, but make sure the screen is covered (with cardboard or other material) until the exact time of the TV announcer's lines.

Ladder and other tools to give an industrial look to The Factory.

Cassette player

The Cross Rectifier Machine must be large enough to walk either behind or through, and it must hide the performers completely from the audience for at least a few seconds. It can be as simple as a blanket draped over a movie screen.

The roving narrator is on stage throughout the entire play. Between his/her parts the narrator moves to a less conspicuous spot on the stage. Of course, the characters are oblivious to the narrator's presence.

The mini-drama opens with all three parties on stage. Alex Pinkerton is reading the paper; his wife is watering a plant. Vince Brown is in his easy chair watching TV (the cardboard box with the announcer inside). The Redfords are playing Monopoly.

Narrator: For decades, social scientists have been trying to develop theories concerning the origin of the human race. We're about to set out on an adventure with six people who, in their own way, are wondering the same thing. Just where *did* they come from?

(Moves toward the Pinkertons.) Meet Alex and Martha Pinkerton. The Pinkertons are, I suppose, what some would call "upper eschelon." Others would call them "snobs."

Alex, after graduating from a prestigious London business school, successfully united his creative approach to economics with his education by forming the World Stock and Bond Investment firm. It had been a hard road, but it could no longer be said that they were found wanting in any of life's necessities. Now they are "society people."

Martha Pinkerton is currently the chairwoman of the local Garden Club and occasionally opens their home to the other members. The weekly meetings include guest lecturers who expound for hours on such topics as the plight of the Egyptian tea rose or effective propagation of rubber trees. Yes, Alex and Martha Pinkerton's contributions to society are surely hard to surpass. Alex just wishes more people would appreciate them. *(Narrator steps to rear of stage.)*

Alex: *(In British accent, frustrated by his reading of a business journal.)* How can these economic bunglers call themselves "experts"? Don't they realize that the deficit is simply too great to expect the trends to continue in a progressive manner? There will be repercussions that only the most insightful analysts, such as myself, could predict. And they call themselves economic "experts"! *(Tosses magazine down.)*

Martha: Now Pinkie, calm down. Remember your blood pressure. I know that you're deeply concerned over the current fiscal problems that face our country, but no amount of undignified behavior will remedy the situation.

Alex: I'm telling you, Luvie, I'm at my wit's end with these foolish analyses and predictions. I don't know what more I can do to call it to the Parliament's attention. Maybe I should just, as the Yankees say, "Let it all hang out." It might work. You know, do something foolish to draw some attention, and then, once I've gained an audience, simply speak my piece.

Martha: *(Shocked.)* Pinkie! Don't even think such thoughts! Remember who you are! You're *not* a Yankee! *(Consoles him now.)* Dear, try to relax. I know how you feel. Even *I* could use a nice, long holiday.

Alex: What's that?

Martha: I said try to relax.

Alex: No, no, the other part.

Martha: I said, "Even *I* could use a holiday." But it was just a silly suggestion. After all, I *do* have the Garden Club meeting next week.

Alex: No, I think you're right. Maybe both of us need to embark on an adventure of some sort to relieve the tensions that plague us and get away from this urban blight. *(Sighs.)* Oh, but Luvie, we must face reality. We've already participated in every possible kind of adventure. We've hunted the darkest African jungle and skied the mightiest mountains. What can there possibly be that we haven't already exhausted our energies on? Maybe we're what the Yanks would call "over the hill." *(Slumps down in resignation, staring at journal on floor.)*

Martha: I've always dreamed of hunting for the elusive wing-petaled variegated orchid along the banks of the—

Alex: *(Interrupting.)* Luvie, look here—in this journal. *(Picks up magazine, intently reading aloud.)* It says, "Trace your line of production. With this innovative kit you can trace your own unique line of production all the way back to the original Factory." Luvie! That's it! The ultimate challenge! *(Now he grows dreamy-eyed.)* To prove our true ancestry, to discover the royal realities of the Pinkerton heritage. We will trod the paths of those who have gone before us. *(Standing, dramatically.)* And we shall not stop until we find The Factory!

Martha: *(Caught up in the moment.)* Pinkie! I've never seen you like this! But surely we couldn't follow through with such a plan! What about the Garden Club meeting next week?

Alex: *(Suddenly loosens up.)* Those old begonias will be here when we get back. Now we must send in six dollars and ninety-eight cents, American currency, to this address. It's some place called "Kingdom Hills, California." Come along, Luvie. We must post this immediately. *(Both exit.)*

Narrator: *(Steps over to Vince Brown, who is making a sandwich.)* Meet Vince Brown. Vince is a bachelor who is currently on vacation from his position as sales representative for Neilson Refrigeration.

Now Vince is normally the kind of guy who would spend his vacation at the beach trying to catch a few rays of sun or a girl, and not necessarily in that order. But this vacation is different. Vince has had something on his mind for a couple of weeks now—his family.

Vince had known for a long time that he was adopted. He'd known that for a long time. But now, as Vince sat thinking, he began to wonder about his *real* family. Who were they? Were they rich? Or were they even alive? Was it possible that he might have a real brother or sister living somewhere? His adopted parents had always put him off when he asked such questions, but now he was on his own. If there were only a way to answer that haunting question. *(Narrator steps back.)*

Vince: *(To himself.)* Well, here it is—vacation time. It looks like this one is going to be an all-time loser. I just can't seem to get this nagging question, about my real family off my mind. I suppose that'll just have to remain one of life's little mysteries. Maybe a tomato sandwich and some mindless entertainment will help me forget about it. *(Flips on TV, sits down.)*

(At this point, the person who has been hiding in the TV pops up and becomes a TV announcer.)

TV Announcer: We'll return to *Killer Tomatoes* in a moment. *(Vince lifts a corner of his sandwich and eyes it suspiciously.)* But first, if you've ever wondered about your family history, here's just the thing for you. *(Holds up a manila envelope.)* It's called the Trace Your Factory Kit. This little packet contains everything you need to answer any question you may have pertaining to your heritage. Yes, now you can solve the ever-present mystery of not knowing which factory you came from. Have you ever been curious to know if you're related to King Tut or Queen Elizabeth? Now is the time to find out. Included in the kit are line-of-production charts, pencils, an information packet, and step-by-step instructions on how to unravel the mystery of your family history. To receive your kit, simply write: *(Vince grabs a pencil.)* "Trace Your Factory Kit," Box J, Kingdom Hills, California 99998. Send today. You'll be glad you did! Now, back to *Killer Tomatoes*.

Vince: *(Jumps up excitedly and turns TV off.)* This is fantastic! I have time off, and if I send this in right away, I can spend some of my vacation working on it. I'm going to get this in the mail right now! It might end up being just what I'm looking for! *(Vince exits.)*

Narrator: *(Moving toward the Redford's living room.)* I suppose you've all been anxiously waiting to drop in on the Redford family. Well, here they are. Meet Curtis, Wilma, and Billie-Lee Redford. They belong to the social class known as the "upland heritage." Some would simply call them "hillbillies."

(The narrator steps toward the rear of the stage. The Redfords are around the table playing a game of Monopoly. All have a strong southern accent.)

Curtis: *(Moves playing piece.)* One, two, three, four. Water Works!

Wilma: *(Upset.)* Where'd you learn how to count?

Curtis: Now don't you start flappin' your lips. You know just as good as I do that I'm on Water Works.

Wilma: *(Irritated.)* Well, whoopee do. Billie-Lee, your move.

Billie-Lee: *(Rolls dice and moves.)* One, two, three.

Wilma: Ha, ha! Go to jail.

Billie-Lee: Shut up, Mama.

Curtis: Billie-Lee, you shut up your own mouth. I arta slap you up the side of your head for talkin' that way to your own mama. Wilma, move, would ya?

Wilma: All right, all right. *(Rolls dice and moves.)* One, two, three, four, five. Yes, sir! Park Place!

Curtis: Aw, come on. You probly moved when I weren't lookin'. I cain't never win at this game. Seems like I cain't never win at nothin'. *(Disgusted.)* Park Place. Well, I'll tell you one thang. *(Stands.)* If I owned me a bunch of them fancy places in *real* life, I wouldn't be alivin' here. No, sir. I'd be alivin' in one of them what they call a "henhouse" apartments. Yes, sir, I would.

Wilma: Aw, Curtis, go on. You don't have to be a talkin' that way just cause I always land on Park Place and you never do.

Curtis: No, I mean it, Wilma. You know we could, too, if'n those uppety-up landlords knew what kind of southern stock we come from. I'm tellin' ya, if they knew that we're kin to some of the greatest heroes the South ever knew, they'da be here knockin' on our door beggin' us to come and live in one of their henhouse apartments. We'd be up there alookin' down on them, instead of them always alookin' down on us.

Wilma: Why, shore, Curtis. But how in this ever-lovin' world would ya hope to prove somethin' like that?

Curtis: I know, Wilma, I know. . . .

(Curtis goes over and flips on the radio, which is actually a cassette tape. This is played over a cassette player or a public address system, whichever is appropriate. The announcer immediately comes in.)

Radio Announcer: *(In southern drawl.)* And those were the Kentucky Thoroughbreds with "The Mason-Dixon Stomp." It's sixty-two degrees outside the WOMP studios. Have ya ever wondered how you could trace your line of production? *(Curtis takes notice.)* It's a mighty simple thang to do with the new Trace Your Factory Kit. About everything ya need ta do is all right in there—line-of-production charts, a couple of pencils, and a whole bunch of instructions. It seems to me that if you're thinkin' about figuring out where ya came from, this here Trace Your Factory Kit is just the ticket. Now what ya need to do is git yourself a pencil *(Curtis gets pencil and starts writing.)* and send off to this here address: "Trace Your Factory Kit," Box J, Kingdom Hills, Califor-ni-a. The zippy code is 99998. Now get a move on, ya hear? And speakin' of gettin' a move on, how about a little flat pickin' from Charlie Byrd? *(Curtis turns the radio off.)*

Curtis: *(Excitedly.)* Did ya hear that, Wilma?

Wilma: *(Sarcastically.)* Yeah, I hear'd that, Wilma. What about it?

Curtis: Don't ya git it? That's what we been awaitin' fer. A way ta prove what kind of southern stock we come from. With that there Trace You a Factory Kit, we can show all them city slickers that we's just as good as them, probly better! I betcha by the time we git them forms in that kit filled out, we'll be afindin' that we got ourselves a line of production that runs di-rectly into that of General Robert E. Lee. *(Curtis salutes.)*

Wilma: Well, firstn' off ya gotta go down to the post office and send in for the crazy thang!

Curtis: Well, c'mon, then. What're we waitin' fer?

(The Redfords exit.)

Narrator: And with that, the Pinkertons, Vince Brown, and the Redford family anxiously awaited the arrival of the Trace Your Factory Kits.

A few days later the kits began showing up in the mail. *(All three parties come back on stage, kits in hand.)* Everyone excitedly opened their kits and found inside just what the advertisements had said. There were line-of-production charts, pencils, and a packet of instructions. In addition, there was an envelope in each kit marked "Special Instructions. Open when deemed necessary." It seemed a bit unusual, but each party simply decided to wait and open the special instructions later. They figured they would know when the time was right.

They all began their adventure by reading the regular packet of instructions. The instructions seemed rather complicated at first. But the parties soon discovered that tracing their respective lines of production wasn't really that hard. They filled in the various charts with the names of their aunts and uncles, grandfathers and grandmothers. Vince seemed to have the most trouble, but he did the best he could. Some of the others had to make long-distance phone calls, which usually paid off.

As they began to fill the charts, it became more difficult to remember the names of distant relatives. The Pinkertons couldn't remember whose side of the family their Great-aunt Matilda was on, while Curtis Redford wasn't sure if Stonewall Hickman was his third cousin or his great uncle. Vince was even more discouraged, as he didn't have much to go on from the start. It looked like they were all quickly heading for a dead end. There was only one thing left to do. They would have to resort to the "Special Instructions."

Having opened the envelopes, the instructions contained inside were found to be a bit mystifying. They spoke of a certain location where each party was to arrive exactly six days from the date they opened the envelope. There was a map included, and pertinent landmarks were noted to assist them along the way. In the vicinity where their journey was to terminate was a spot simply marked "The Factory," where they would find the necessary information to complete their individual line-of-production charts.

At first they wondered if the entire escapade might just be an elaborate hoax. But the thought of being able to prove their true ancestry overruled their sense of uncertainty. Eventually everyone decided to make the journey. They would take the risk, hoping to discover "The Factory."

(All exit except the narrator. If a curtain is available, it should close at this point while The Factory props are put into place. If there is no curtain, the focus will shift momentarily to the area where the Cross Rectifier Machine and the various industrial props have been located.)

Narrator: Toward the beginning of the trip, everyone had a certain sense of determination. The Pinkertons were dedicated to proving their royal line of production, while Vince Brown had a renewed enthusiasm for settling the issue on his mind. Curtis Redford wanted to live in a "henhouse" apartment. So on the various groups traveled.

After four days, the momentum had begun to wane. All were tired and irritable, but they decided that they had come too far to turn back. They just hoped that it would be worth the long hours of travel.

The sixth day finally *did* arrive, and it was just about noon when, nearing what was believed to be the destination of their journey, a couple of familiar voices could be heard.

(At this point the narrator exits. If there is a curtain, it reopens. Otherwise, the focus now shifts to The Factory area.)

Alex: *(Discouraged and tired.)* Oh, Luvie. Perhaps we should have turned back. I feel exceptionally foolish having fallen into such a— *(Pauses, looks toward The Factory.)* Luvie, look! *(Points.)*

Martha: Oh, dear! What *is* that odd-looking structure?

Alex: I'm not really sure. It appears to be some sort of abandoned industrial facility.

Martha: Oh, Alex. I don't know if we should go near that. It might be unsafe.

Alex: I suppose you're right. But I'm afraid my adventurous instincts have been aroused. Let's just take a closer look.

(The Pinkertons slowly walk over toward The Factory area.)

Alex: Luvie! What have we stumbled onto here?

Martha: Alex! Look above the door. The sign says, "Enter here for museum tour." This doesn't make any sense at all!

Alex: *(Determined.)* I'm going inside. We may be about to discover something of tremendous significance.

Martha: *(Hesitant.)* If you insist. But we must be careful.

(The Pinkertons enter The Factory.)

Alex: It's so dark in here. Look at all of these pictures hanging on the walls. They appear to be drawings of this facility when it was in use.

(A voice comes from outside.)

Vince: *(From off stage.)* Hey! is anybody in there?

Alex: *(Startled.)* Why, yes, but we intend to do no harm.

(Vince enters The Factory.)

Vince: What are you people doing in here?

Alex: *(Regaining composure.)* And I might ask you the same.

Vince: I'm sorry. My name is Vince Brown, and if I tried to explain to you what I'm doing here, you probably wouldn't believe me.

Alex: I must say it *is* a bit unusual.

Vince: By the way, what exactly brings *you* here?

(Another voice comes from outside The Factory.)

Curtis: *(Off stage, shouting.)* Wilma! You ain't gonna believe what crazy thang I found a yonder. Git over here!

(Curtis slowly enters. Wilma and Billie-Lee follow shortly.)

Alex: Oh, this is absurd. What form of so-called human life do we have here now?

Curtis: What in tarnation's goin' on here?

(All start to speak at once; confusion sets in.)

Vince: *(Finally.)* Hey! Quiet everybody! *(Everyone quiets down.)* Thank you. I'd like to at least explain to all of you what *I'm* doing here. You see, I have reason to believe that I may have a long-lost brother or possibly a sister that I've never seen. I came here on a long-shot hoping to discover his or her whereabouts.

Curtis: Well, if ya ain't never seen 'em, how are ya gonna know it's them? And what makes ya think they'd be alivin' in here?

(The group again grows loud; confusion sets in once more. At this point, the Foreman enters, dressed in a white lab coat.)

Foreman: Excuse me. *(The group quiets down.)* If I'm not mistaken, you folks must be here for the museum tour. Welcome to The Factory. And congratulations on seeing your project through. Many people give up before they've even opened the Special Instructions envelope.

Alex: My good man, what is going on here? And what do you know about the Special Instructions envelope?

Foreman: If you will all gather around, I'll explain everything. *(Everyone draws closer.)* You see, the place at which you've arrived is the original Factory. The various lines of production began right here. And that is the object of your search, is it not?

(All nod in agreement.)

Vince: But when you say the "various" lines of production began here, you must mean that "some" of our lines of production originated here. You have to admit that we're all very different.

Alex: *(Looking at Curtis.)* To say the least.

Foreman: In one sense, yes. It's true that each line of production has distinct characteristics. But to say that one line of production, for example, the Pinkerton's, is superior to another, say, the Redford's, is a distortion of the facts.

Curtis: Hot dog! Did ya hear that, Wilma?

Alex: Have mercy!

Martha: It sounds to me as if this has simply turned out to be a wasted effort. We came here hoping to prove that ours is a royal line of production.

Foreman: We are not here to *prove* anything. Rather, I am hoping to *provide* you with a new perspective on life. Yours is in fact a very royal line of production, headed by the greatest King who ever lived.

Alex: Hot dog! *(Quickly regains his reserve.)* What I mean is, your statement seems to support my convictions.

Vince: But what about me? How does all this relate to *my* search? Do you know if I have a brother or sister living somewhere?

Curtis: And what about me? Am I a kin to General Lee?

Foreman: I'm beginning to see that there is only one way to lay all of your questions to rest. Follow me. *(The whole group walks over to the Cross Rectifier Machine.)* This machine was designed specifically to allow people such as yourselves to see things as they really are. It is called the Cross Rectifier Machine. Admittedly, it, along with The Factory itself, appears to be a little worn out. But I prefer to think of them as being "well-used." People have been making the same journey you've made for many years. Inevitably, the easiest way to provide the answers they're looking for is to show them this machine. Those who attain a genuine understanding of what the machine was designed to accomplish learn an eternal truth.

Wilma: I ain't never seen such a funny lookin' contraption.

Foreman: But one should never underestimate the internal worth of something or someone. Perhaps the greatest favor I can do for all of you is to simply allow you to experience the results of the machine for yourselves. If you'll simply enter here *(Points.)*, I believe you will discover much more than you ever dreamed of when you began your journey. Perhaps the Pinkertons would like to be first.

Alex: *(Martha looks hesitant. Alex speaks.)* Never let it be said that a Pinkerton had a cowardly streak. *(He starts to enter, followed by Martha.)*

100   Creative Skits for Youth Groups

Foreman: *(Just before they step in.)* I should offer one word of caution. Shortly after you leave the machine, you will experience a period of color blindness. How long it lasts is up to you.

(The Pinkertons look at each other briefly then enter the Cross Rectifer Machine. The Foreman steps over and starts the machine. He then shows Vince Brown the way. The Redford family follows and the Foreman exits. This is a particularly important part of the mini-drama. Then, as each person goes behind, or through, the machine, he or she removes his or her respective color patches. This symbolizes the removal of prejudices. As they exit the machine, the actors and actresses, except for Billie-Lee, must be careful to avoid looking at each other directly for a short period of time. Rather, they speak as if to themselves.)

Alex: *(As he exits the machine.)* My, what an exhilarating experience!

Martha: It was an unusual sensation, wasn't it?

Vince: Very interesting. Maybe now the Foreman will tell me about my brother or sister.

Billie-Lee: *(Looks at the Pinkertons and Vince, then shouts back to Wilma.)* Mama!

Wilma: Hush up your mouth, Billie-Lee. Curtis, are you comin'?

Curtis: Yeah, I'ma comin'. I'm gonna have me a talk with that there Foreman. I think he done pulled a fast one on us.

Billie-Lee: But Mama!

Wilma: Billie-Lee, now you hush on up, ya hear?

Vince: Hey, where did the Foreman go?

Alex: I should have guessed it! This is all somebody's idea of a publicity stunt.

Martha: But he seemed sincere.

Billie-Lee: *(Shouts.)* Mama!

Wilma: Billie-Lee Redford, would you shut up your mouth for two minutes?

Billie-Lee: But, Mama, don't ya see anything different since y'all went through that machine?

Wilma: What're you talkin' about?

Billie-Lee: Before we all went into that machine, we was all different. But look! *(Points to everyone's cheeks.)* We's all the same now!

(Everyone looks at each other in astonishment and mumbles to himself or herself in a state of shock.)

Vince: The Cross Rectifier! That's what did it! That's what the Foreman meant by being "color blind"!

Alex: I think I finally understand! Somewhere, far back in our lines of production, we *did* all come from the same Factory!

Martha: If that's the case, Pinkie, then we really *do* come from a royal line of production!

Alex: *(Thoughtful.)* In more ways than one, Luvie, in more ways than one.

Vince: This is fantastic. This lays to rest for good my question about having a brother or sister. Of course I do. I have a whole world full of them!

Curtis: Oh, I git ya. So I really is a kin to Robert E. Lee.

Wilma: True, Curtis. But it also means you's a kin to Ulysses S. Grant.

Curtis: *(More gently.)* Now hush up your mouth, Wilma.

Vince: What it *really* means is that we're all a kin to each other.

Martha: But what about the Foreman—who was he?

Vince: I have a feeling that he's the one who was responsible for arranging this whole trip. He seemed to know too much about us for this to be a fluke.

Alex: Whoever he was, we owe him a debt of gratitude.

Curtis: I'll tell ya one thang. That there Foreman is a workin' man. I could tell by his hands. He even had a couple of scars in 'em. That's a sign of a man who ain't afraid ta tackle a job.

Vince: Something tells me we'll all have the chance to thank him someday. But don't forget Billie-Lee here. She's the one who first noticed it. I guess it would pay us all to see things through a child's eyes once in a while.

Alex: Well, ladies and gentlemen, I believe we have met the ultimate challenge. We have indeed discovered our *true* heritage.

Vince: I suppose we might as well head back. This is really going to be something to tell the guys back at the refrigeration company. I have the feeling that the more people who hear about this, the better off we'll all be. Well, so long, family!

(All begin to leave, but just then Curtis interrupts them.)

Curtis: Just a minute there. I just thought of somethin' that's kinda profound. That don't happen too often with me.

Wilma: What in this ever-lovin' world are ya talkin' about?

Curtis: Well, all I kin say is one thang. It just goes to show that we's all meat from the same bone!

(All chuckle. Vince puts his arm around Curtis.)

Vince: Well said, brother, well said. *(Leading the way.)* Come on, everybody. Let's go home!

(All walk out, preferably down an aisle and through a rear exit. A song on unity might be played while they are walking out.)

Suggested Scripture

Psalm 133; Luke 10:29–37; Acts 10:34–35; Ephesians 2:14, 19–22